C. S. Lewis in 1947. *Photograph by A. P. Strong*

Through Joy and Beyond

A PICTORIAL BIOGRAPHY

OF

C. S. LEWIS

WALTER HOOPER

MACMILLAN PUBLISHING CO., INC.

NEW YORK

COLLIER MACMILLAN PUBLISHERS

LONDON

Macmillan Publishing Co., Inc.
866 Third Avenue, New York, N.Y. 10022
Collier Macmillan Canada, Inc.

Library of Congress Cataloging in Publication Data

Hooper, Walter.
Through joy and beyond.

Bibliography: p.
Includes index.
1. Lewis, C. S. (Clive Staples), 1898–1963—
Biography. 2. Lewis, C. S. (Clive Staples), 1898–
1963—Portraits, etc. 3. Authors, English—20th
century—Biography. I. Title.
PR6023.E926Z677 1982   828′.91209 [B]   82-9884
ISBN 0-02-553670-2   AACR2

10   9   8   7   6   5   4   3   2   1

Printed in the United States of America

Grateful acknowledgment is made for permission to reproduce materials as follows:

Excerpts from SURPRISED BY JOY: The Shape of My Early Life by C. S. Lewis are reprinted by permission of Harcourt Brace Jovanovich, Inc. and by William Collins Publishers; © copyright 1955 by C. S. Lewis PTE Limited.

Excerpts from Letters of C. S. Lewis, edited by W. H. Lewis, are reprinted by permission of Harcourt Brace Jovanovich, Inc. and by William Collins Publishers; © copyright 1966 by W. H. Lewis and C. S. Lewis PTE Limited.

Photographs from LETTERS OF C. S. LEWIS, edited by W. H. Lewis, copyright © 1966 by W. H. Lewis and C. S. Lewis PTE Limited. Reproduced by permission of Harcourt Brace Jovanovich, Inc.

Excerpts from They Stand Together: The Letters of C. S. Lewis to Arthur Greeves, edited by Walter Hooper, reprinted by permission of Macmillan Publishing Co., Inc., and William Collins Publishers. Text copyright © 1979 by C. S. Lewis PTE Limited. Introduction and notes © copyright 1979 by Walter Hooper.

"Oxford," from Spirits in Bondage, 1919, C. S. Lewis PTE Limited.

The cover of TIME for September 8, 1947, copyright 1947, Time Inc. All rights reserved. Reprinted by permission from TIME.

Contents

INTRODUCTION
The Book and the Film

THE ORIGINS of this pictorial biography go back to the morning of September 14, 1977, when I was on holiday. Exhausted from the many years spent editing a still unfinished six-hundred-page volume of C. S. Lewis's letters, I was, like Uncle Remus's Brer Rabbit, "layin' low." But not so low that Mr. Bob O'Donnell, a film producer and long a friend to the Lewis estate, did not discover my whereabouts and telephone me. He enquired about the possibility of filming one of Lewis's books. As *The Lion, the Witch and the Wardrobe* was already being filmed, and as other of Lewis's books were under option, I suggested that a better idea might be to make a documentary film of Lewis's life. All the same, I hoped he would not spring into action too soon, as I knew all too well his passion for hard work. I was relieved when he said he should need to give it some thought; then a little terrified when he said he'd ring me again in five minutes with his answer. "Surely," I said, "you mean five days or even five months?" But Bob O'Donnell—as I see from my diary —rang precisely five minutes later to say yes, it *would* be a documentary. And as he talked, his enthusiasm was so contagious that by the time he was done I had agreed to write a film script as well as act as narrator. But if I was to finish editing the Lewis–Greeves correspondence—now published as *They Stand Together* (1979)—I might need help.

Back in Oxford I talked it over with my friend Dr. Anthony Marchington of Brasenose College. We shared an admiration for Lewis and a love for simple, clean, English prose. As well, we disliked intensely the use most film-makers had made of Oxford. "Collages" are more in their line than colleges; and they love to suggest that the University is composed almost entirely of amiable lunatics. Much of Bob

O'Donnell's film would be shot in Oxford. Could we see that *he* did it justice? One of the biggest problems to be overcome was permission to film inside the colleges, and as Marchington was a resident member of the University and as interested as I was in a good script, I asked for his help. So it was that when Bob O'Donnell arrived in Oxford on March 13, 1978, we laid our plans before him, and Marchington was urged to join the team as his assistant.

The next day we had a long session in London with Michael Samuelson of Samuelson Film Service Ltd. He promised to provide a film crew, to work under Mr. Terry Gould, whom Bob O'Donnell chose as his production manager. From the first it had been Bob O'Donnell's wish to engage Peter Ustinov as the "voice" of C. S. Lewis, and plans were made to approach him about this. While those negotiations were going on—no one could foresee how Peter Ustinov would respond to the proposal—Terry Gould began selecting the film crew. Some shots would require two or even three crews, but here I think it enough to express our gratitude to those who formed the permanent one: Michael Delaney, the lighting cameraman; Paul Hennesy, the camera operator; David Johnson, the clapper/loader; Charles Frater, the recordist; Joe Vanstone, the driver/grip; Terry Goddard, the gaffer electrician; and Lewis Fawcett, the film editor, who remained in London to judge and report on the "rushes"—those portions of film sent to him every evening.

Because the University was to "break up" for the summer vacation on June 17, and full-time filming was not to begin till July 10, some of the most difficult scenes had to be filmed ahead of schedule and before there was a complete script. This meant that Marchington and I had to write something for me to say on my first appearance in front of the cameras in the Cloister of Magdalen College on May 10. That same day a triple crew was there to light Magdalen College Chapel and film the choristers of Magdalen College School singing that ravishingly beautiful anthem—"I was glad"—by the former Oxford Professor of Music, C. H. H. Parry.

The script was completed on June 10. As Marchington and I were the only ones who knew Oxford well, I see that in it we attempted to describe, as best as we knew how, what the cameras would be filming while Peter Ustinov (or whoever was to be Lewis's "voice") and I talked. It was then, first, that the idea of this book was conceived. The film would require numerous photographs of C. S. Lewis, and as I had for years been collecting photos of my old friend, I saw how the making of the film could serve as an opportunity for using those I had as well as for collecting others—in particular photos of the Lewis family home, "Little Lea," in Belfast and other places associated with his early life. Bob O'Donnell liked the idea of the book, and for this reason we decided to make the documentary as historically accurate as possible, while at the same time taking as many still photos as we might need for a book. Billett Potter was hired to take many of the stills in and around Oxford, and Bob O'Donnell took the rest.

It was for me a particularly special day when, on July 19, we went to film a short sequence in Bristol in front of the house where Lewis spent the last weekend with the Moores before he left for the war in France. And that same day, I see from my diary, turned out to be one of immense relief for Bob O'Donnell. Besides all his work directing the film, we knew he could not fully relax till he knew whether or not Peter Ustinov would agree to be Lewis's "voice." Returning from Bristol, we stopped to film one of Lewis's favourite pubs, "The Trout," at Godstow near Oxford. That being the end of filming for the day, we went in for refreshments. As usual, Bob O'Donnell rang Samuelson's, and it is not likely that any of us will forget the moment he came in and regaled us with the news that Peter Ustinov had accepted.

The next anxiety was, what success, if any, we might have when we crossed to Belfast on July 31? We could not have been more fortunate. Mr. Dennis Rodgers, a building contractor, had bought Little Lea with the purpose of modernising and moving into it himself. This generous man offered to leave it as it was till we had made the only film that could ever be made in it before it was changed forever. But how could we film in a completely empty house? One of Lewis's favourite cousins, Gundreda Ewart Forrest, daughter of Sir William Quartus Ewart, had died some months earlier at the family home, Glenmachan House. Plans were being made for the sale of the house and many of the furnishings. Yet Mrs. Forrest's daughter, Mrs. Primrose Henderson— understanding our problem—allowed us to furnish Little Lea with whatever we needed from Glenmachan: furnishings that would have been almost as familiar to Lewis as those that had been in his own home. It was Mrs. Henderson also who directed us to the spot in the Holywood Hills so beloved of C. S. Lewis.

It was on this spot that I stood before the cameras three times on August 5 and described what I said I could see—the Antrim Mountains, Belfast, and the plain of Down. "Said," because everything except the small area around me was shrouded in a mist impenetrable by the camera. This was a hard blow for all of us and, while I was flown back to England that evening, Bob O'Donnell felt strongly that he should hang on with the crew till the next day. After weeks of mist the sun shone brilliantly the next morning, August 6, and they rushed back to the Holywood Hills to film what before had been little more than a blur. But following on the heels of this report telephoned to me from Belfast came the shattering news that the saintly Pope Paul VI had died.

Even so, Bob O'Donnell and his wife C. A., along with Terry Gould and Charles Frater, had to fly to Rome on the seventh if they were to meet Peter Ustinov in Palermo, Sicily, on August 8. Getting through Rome during this period of mourning was difficult and made more so when all the recording equipment got stuck in Italian customs. As ever, Terry Gould's almost magical qualities of persuasion prevailed and the company, with all the equipment, arrived at Peter Ustinov's hotel on the evening of the eighth. He saw how exhausted they were and suggested that the recording be delayed till the next morning. An improvised studio was set up in his hotel that evening. And, as for the rest, I have it on Bob O'Donnell's authority that not only had Peter Ustinov gone over the script and some tapes of Lewis's voice very carefully, but that in the recording session the following morning even the kindest compliments I have heard paid him fall short of what a wise, charming, and obliging man he is. The film, so enhanced by his voice, was edited by Lewis Fawcett and Bob O'Donnell in the latter's studios of Lord and King Associates of West Chicago, after which it went into world-wide distribution with its premier showing on February 27, 1979. The original version of *Through Joy and Beyond* is composed of three fifty-minute parts: "The Formative Years," "The Informed Years," and "Jack Remembered." Those reminiscences found in this book of Martin Moynihan, Owen Barfield, Robert Havard, Priscilla and Father John Tolkien, and Miss Pauline Baynes were taken from "Jack Remembered."

As I have tried to show, the film and this book are parts of one adventure. But, while it is hoped that those who have seen, or might see, the film will benefit from the story told here, the reader must not suppose them to be the same. This is not the "Book of the Film," far from it. When I stood in front of the cameras in the Cloister of Magdalen and began "Here I am . . ." I knew one could not put such things in a book: that a film and a book fall into different *genres*. At the same time, with so many hundreds of photographs to choose from, the story of

Lewis's life had to be kept fairly short if the book was not to be too expensive to publish.

Long before any of the things described above began, it had been one of my responsibilities as a trustee of the Lewis estate to answer the many letters of appreciation received from Lewis's admirers. Perhaps the most striking feature of these letters is the feeling that the writers know Lewis, and wish to know him better. Having myself known the books before I knew the man, I do not think they are deceived. Lewis was indeed very like the man we meet in his books. It was not deliberate on his part, but I think he was aware of it nonetheless. I don't imagine he was thinking of it when he wrote a preface to his friend Austin Farrer's book *A Faith of Our Own* (1960). Even so, it seems to me that one of the things he noticed in Farrer's writings is uncannily true of Lewis himself. Dr. Farrer, he said, "is never speaking to the abstraction 'modern man'; always to you and me, whom he seems to know sufficiently well. That is how—unobtrusively, and with all respect for the individual mysteries we are—he gets under our skin . . . To talk to us thus Dr. Farrer makes himself almost nothing, almost nobody. To be sure, in the event, his personality stands out from the pages as clearly as that of any author; but this is one of heaven's jokes—nothing makes a man so noticeable as vanishing."

Lewis's admirers—or many of them—want to *see* as well as meet him, and this book was compiled for those who ask to see as much as possible of one they feel they already know. In choosing the photographs I thought would do the most to make this a comfortable, relaxing, and celebrative book, I was reminded of the delight Lewis took in the stories of Uncle Remus. Once when he was sitting before the fire with his feet on the fender, he asked me to read aloud the one called "A Dream and a Story." Uncle Remus says that it is often when he "sets en dozes" against "de chimbley-jam" that Brer Rabbit and all the other "creeturs come slippin' in on des tiptoes . . . en get up a reg'lar juberlee."

Those who have helped make this book a "reg'lar juberlee" are too numerous to name here, but particular thanks must go to my friend Anthony Marchington, who helped so much with the film script. It was my bad luck that he moved from Oxford before this book began to take form. I am also indebted to my co-trustee Owen Barfield, and Lewis's cousin Mrs. Beth Tate. She is the daughter of the distinguished blood specialist, Dr. Joseph Lewis (1898–1969), who attended Lewis's father in his last illness and who often looked after Lewis. Amongst other things, she has supplied me with the only photos I have seen of both Lewis's great-grandparents, Mr. and Mrs. Joseph Lewis, as well as some early photographs of Lewis's parents.

I suppose it is a rare treat when an author finds his publisher as interested in the subject of his book as he is. But it happened with me. My fear of New York City was shaken off when, in her office in one of the largest buildings I've been in, Miss Jane Cullen of Macmillan Publishing Co.—with as much sense and sensibility as the other Jane—poured out cup after cup of tea as we threw our energy into the difficult task of interweaving the photographs with the written words.

I would have been justified in dedicating this book to the British actor, Michael York, for his splendid recordings of some of Lewis's books. I do so because he is a man whose friendship I value very, very much. He is one of the many who have asked me for a photograph of Lewis. I hope he and all the others find what they want here.

WALTER HOOPER

Oxford
November 22, 1981

PART I

Early Years

The Mountains of Mourne

THIS STORY STARTS IN IRELAND, on the Mountains of Mourne in fact, and things don't change much up there—away from it all where the wind blows. And it's where this tale ends too, if these things ever end. For this story has that simple truth about it.

At the beginning of this century, and the place has seen many a hard winter and forgotten summer's day since then, a little lad used to go up there on his holidays; and there he savoured alone the bitter-sweet longing for desire which he later called Joy. For he knew it to be an experience common in a greater or lesser extent to all men. This story testifies to that Joy and tells of the man who came to know it for what it was, who gave it the familiar ring of truth. That little lad, you see, was C. S. Lewis, destined to become one of the finest Christian Apologists of our time. The first man to glance through Joy and beyond.

Out to the east the Mountains of Mourne "sweep down to the sea." In the west, Newry, and beyond, quiet lanes with legends of highway-men. Now north and over the moorside a lot farther than you can see is Belfast.

Belfast for Lewis was a different place than it is today, but one place as yet unaltered lies on the Holywood Hills above the city. From there one can gaze across to the Antrim Mountains, on a summer's day a uniform mass of greyish blue. That for Lewis was one beauty and the Holywood Hills themselves were another, quite different, and even for him more dearly loved, for it was grassy there and dewy. But down on the valley floor is another story. Belfast Lough is, and remains, a forest of factory chimneys, gantries, and giant cranes rising out of a welter of a mist.

But for all this, thoughts of the Mountains of Mourne were never

[3]

far away, and across the fields and the lane over onto the top of the bank on the far side, the clamour of the city is behind you. Of this view Lewis wrote, "And having seen it, blame me if you can for being a romantic. For here is the thing itself, utterly irresistible, the way to the world's end, the land of longing, the breaking and blessing of hearts."[1] This is the plain of Down.

Clive Staples Lewis was born in the now extinct semi-detached house "Dundela Villas" on the outskirts of Belfast on November 29, 1898. The house is recorded by a sole surviving picture. His father, Albert Lewis, was of Welsh farming stock, for his father before him had

The Plain of Down seen from the Holywood Hills

Joseph Lewis, great-
grandfather of CSL

come over from Wales and worked himself up into a successful engineering partnership—"MacIlwaine and Lewis: Boiler Makers, Engineers and Iron Ship Builders"—a fine company which, like its name and the ships it produced, testified to all that base eloquence of nineteenth-century industry. Lewis was later to describe his grandfather as "a self-made man"[2] and certainly Richard Lewis's success in private business was to benefit particularly his youngest son, Albert, who received a more elaborate education than had been bestowed on any of his three brothers.

Whether it was because of Albert's precocity or the rising fortunes of the family, his education was to be more far-reaching than could have been imagined. For after leaving the District Model National School he went in 1877, at fourteen, to Lurgan College in County Armagh and so to the headmaster there, William T. Kirkpatrick. It's often interesting how things turn out and we will hear of Kirkpatrick— the "Great Knock" as the Lewises called him—later on. Save to say that Albert Lewis was taken under his wing and after qualifying as a solicitor with distinction in 1885 he had a brief partnership and then started a practice of his own in Belfast, which he conducted with uniform success for the rest of his life.

Richard Lewis,
grandfather of CSL

Martha Gee Lewis,
grandmother of CSL

In 1894 Albert Lewis had then another little success, for after years of trying he married Flora, the daughter of the Reverend Thomas Hamilton, the local rector at St. Mark's, Dundela. The Lewises were parishioners there. The Hamiltons were of a nobly ecclesiastical stock and Flora was by any standard a cool-headed woman with a First in mathematics from Queen's College, Belfast. Never had a Jacob served more arduously for his Rachel than did Albert. After eight years of persistent courtship she wrote: "I wonder do I love you? I am not quite sure. I know that at least I am very fond of you, and that I should never think of loving anyone else."[3]

They were married in St. Mark's on August 29, 1894. Flora's father, the rector, had long held Albert as a favourite and they regularly tripped about together. At the reception afterwards he was heard to say, somewhat disappointedly, "Now that he's got what he wanted, there'll be no more jaunts."[4] It's a quiet little church still—designed by the famous architect, Butterfield, in fact—and it makes you wonder: none of the guests, not even the bride or groom, could have had any idea as to where it was all leading.

After a honeymoon they settled at Dundela Villas, and not a year later, on June 16, 1895, came their first son, Warren, or "Warnie" as they called him. Three years after that he was followed by Clive Staples, or "Jack" as he preferred to be called from the age of four onwards.

In 1905, when Jack was seven, the first great change in his life occurred. His father with the increasing prosperity had the "New House" built. It is a large house called Little Lea and stood way out in what was then the country, and the Lewis boys liked it. As Jack said later, it was badly designed and constructed with draughts in every room, but it was large and filled with books. And the view over the fields to the Castlereagh Hills was distant yet beckoning.

Jack and Warnie were as close as ever, for these were the "golden years" before all the changes, and on windy days big and little brother would set off on their bicycles and seek a way into the rural quiet with thoughts of a chance meeting with a knight in full plate or a leprechaun with a pot of gold.

The house was indeed spacious and when the Irish weather drove them inside they'd find attics to explore. "I am a product of long corridors," said Lewis, "empty sunlit rooms, upstair indoor silences, attics explored in solitude, distant noises of gurgling cisterns and pipes, and the noise of wind under the tiles. Also, of endless books. My father bought all the books he read and never got rid of any of them. There were books in the study, books in the drawing room, books in the cloakroom, books (two deep) in the great bookcase on the landing, books in a bedroom, books piled as high as my shoulder in the cistern attic, books of all kinds reflecting every transient stage of my parents' interests, books readable and unreadable, books suitable for a child and books most emphatically not. Nothing was forbidden me. In the seemingly endless rainy afternoons I took volume after volume from the shelves. I had always the same certainty of finding a book that was new to me as a man who walks into a field has of finding a new blade of grass."[5]

In fact a small gable attic—the "little end room"—was his favourite, and the place where the brothers came to make things and be away from everyone. Both of them suffered, however, from a manual clumsiness owing to an inherited deformity of the thumb, and rather than make castles and ships, Lewis was forced to describe them. First came "Animal-Land," embellished with Arthurian mice with swords in full armed combat with gigantic cats. But Warren was to have his influence in this world as well, and "Animal-Land" was soon discovered to be a close neighbour of India, the two being connected with a complex system of shipping routes across the "Burrington Straits." The combination resulted in Jack's (as yet unpublished) stories of the imaginary world of Boxen and characters like James Bar, a bear; Macgoullah, a horse; Viscount Puddiphat, an owl; Their Majesties Benjamin VI and Hawki IV, both rabbits; and—most endearing of all—there is Lord Big, the Prime Minister, who is a frog of immense personality. "In my daydreams," Lewis was later to write, "I was training myself to be a fool; in mapping and chronicling Animal-Land I was training myself to be a novelist."[6] Indeed he was. In a later story from Boxen, *The Locked Door*, we are guests at a special gathering in The Palace:

Great was the preparation of Bar and Macgoullah when the eventful evening arrived. Bar had hired a handsome to be ready for them both outside the "Schooner" where they had arranged to meet.

As they drew near the palace, Regency Street became a mass of moving lights dancing to the music of horses' hoofs and the powerful purr of motors: and it was not without difficulty that the hireling Jehu navigated them to the portals of Regency St. Palace. Stepping out they were conducted by suave domestics to the cloak room, which, as is usually the case on these occasions, was crowded with knots of whispering guests fiddling with their gloves. There of course is Puddiphat immaculately clad; there is Reginald Pig the Shipowner dressed in solid and plain evening dress; there is Quicksteppe looking finer than ever as the electric light catches his glossy curling locks; there is Colonel

Albert Lewis on qualifying
as a solicitor, 1885

Flora Lewis, 1895

Albert Lewis, 1894

Chutney, formerly head of the war office, but now removed to give place to Fortescue who is also present. After some time of nervous fumbling and hushing, Pig, the most couragious person present, led a sort of forlorn hope to the salon where their Majesties were recieving their guests and where stout domestics dispensed tea etc. The two kings were throwing all their histrionic powers into an imitation of enjoyment, and behind them stood the Little-Master looking rather worried. The boys kept up a continual flow of conversation:

"Good evening, my dear Pig! How are the ships? Ah, Viscount Puddiphat, very glad you came."

"Good evening Your Majesties. Ah my dear Little-Master I see you've been having busy times in the Clique"

"Yes" said Big drily

The Duchess of Penzly came up, a heavy woman whom they all abominated.

"Good evening Duchess. Hasn't Miss Penzley—oh! Influenza? I am very sorrey to hear that" The Duchess passed on to Big,

"Ah, Lord Big, this is a pleasure. How delighted I was to hear you had had some excitement in politics, it does liven things up so, doesn't it?"

"It certainly does," responded the frog brusquely, and engaged a dance.[7]

Flora with one of her boys

And just listen to this:

On a certain spring morning, the viscount's valet had entered his master's bedchamber with a cup of chocolate, and the ironed morning paper. No sooner had his step resounded on the floor than a mass of feathers stirred in the large bed, and the owl raised himself on his elbow, with blinking eyes.[8]

There was so much of his father's conversation in these stories, so much of Victorian smoking rooms and railway stations, morning papers and politics. So much of what, ironically, Lewis in fact came later to detest. But there was no doubting that the young Jack Lewis had an outstanding literary ability and an even-tempered rhetoric which for a small boy amounted to extraordinary promise.

This is borne out by an event which happened in 1907 when the family were in preparation for a forthcoming holiday in France. His brother later wrote of it: "The trip to France—our last holiday with our mother—materialised and it was no doubt whilst it was under discussion that Jack first showed that dexterity in riposte for which he was to become famous. Entering the study, where my father was poring over his account books, he flung himself into a chair and observed, 'I have a

Albert Lewis, 1898

prejudice against the French.' My father, interrupted in a long addition sum, said irritably, 'Why?' Jack, crossing his legs and putting his finger tips together, replied, 'If I knew *why* it would not be a prejudice.' "9

On another occasion there occurred the incident of Mrs. Mop and the dinner—a whimsical prank of Jack's which passed into the Lewis family history. Mrs. Mop was the charwoman. It came about that all the other house servants—they had half a dozen or so—were absent in the middle of the day. So it fell to Mrs. Mop to cook the meal. Boys are supposed to be able to eat anything; but raw steak, lightly browned on the outside, flanked by potatoes which had apparently been immersed in warm water for a couple of minutes defeated them. "Let us," said Jack, "give this mess a ceremonial funeral." No sooner said than done. Outside the kitchen window was a flower bed and at the table was Mrs. Mop having her own dinner. They advanced on the flower bed in Indian file at a slow pace, Jack in front carrying the gramophone playing Chopin's "Funeral March," Warnie following with a trowel in one hand and the dinner in the other. A grave was dug, the meal buried, and after a minute's reverent silence they withdrew to the house in the order in which they had come, the gramophone still playing. Mrs. Mop was so enraged that she flounced out of the house immediately and they never saw her again.

But a little lad with such a fine intellect didn't spend all his time inventing stories of an imaginary world. No, there were other times, and increasingly now, when his imagination took him and held him just for a moment effortlessly and without warning. It was the glimpse of promised genius, the quiet ecstasy of utter givenness which he sought with a desirous innocence. And yet it brought its loneliness, for as Wordsworth in *The Prelude* wrote:

> In November days,
> When vapours rolling down the valley made
> A lonely scene more lonesome, among woods,
> At noon and 'mid the calm of summer nights,
> When, by the margin of the trembling lake,
> Beneath the gloomy hills homeward I went
> In solitude, such intercourse was mine;
> Mine was it in the fields both day and night,
> And by the waters, all the summer long.
>
> (Bk. I, 416–24)

And the young Lewis had it too—though his family couldn't have known it. The responsibility was that little lad's alone. He was the one, as the poet went on to say, "Surprised by Joy—impatient as the wind." And although he didn't understand it at the time, it was to be the most important experience of his life:

It will be clear that . . . I was living almost entirely in my imagination: or at least that the imaginative experience of those years now seems to me more

C. S. Lewis in childhood

Lurgan College

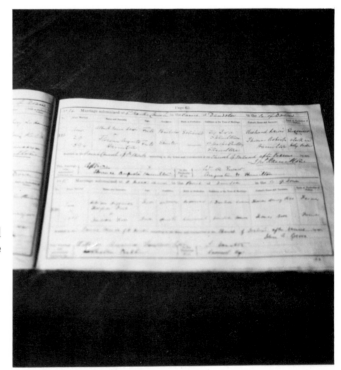

Register of Albert and
Flora's marriage

Cartoon of Albert Lewis in 1892

Register of CSL's baptism

important than anything else . . . The first is itself the memory of a memory. As I stood beside a flowering currant bush on a summer day there suddenly arose in me without warning, and as if from a depth not of years but of centuries, the memory of that earlier morning at the Old House when my brother had brought his toy garden into the nursery. It is difficult to find words strong enough for the sensation which came over me; Milton's "enormous bliss" of Eden . . . comes somewhere near it. It was a sensation, of course, of desire; but desire for what? not, certainly, for a biscuit-tin filled with moss, nor even . . . for my own past . . . Before I knew what I desired, the desire itself was gone, the whole glimpse withdrawn, the world turned commonplace again, or only stirred by a longing for the longing that had just ceased. It had taken only a moment of time; and in a certain sense everything else that had ever happened to me was insignificant in comparison.

The second glimpse came through *Squirrel Nutkin;* through it only, though I loved all the Beatrix Potter books. But . . . it administered the shock, it was a trouble. It troubled me with what I can only describe as the idea of Autumn . . . The experience was one of intense desire . . . and in this experience also there was the same surprise and the same sense of incalculable importance . . .

The third glimpse came through poetry. I had become fond of Longfellow's *Saga of King Olaf:* fond of it in a casual, shallow way for its story and its vigorous rhythms. But then, and quite different from such pleasures, and like a voice from far more distant regions, there came a moment when I idly turned the pages of the book and found the unrhymed translation of *Tegner's Drapa* and read

> *I heard a voice that cried,*
> *Balder the beautiful*
> *Is dead, is dead—*

I knew nothing about Balder; but instantly I was uplifted into huge regions of northern sky, I desired with almost sickening intensity something never to be described (except that it is cold, spacious, severe, pale and remote) and then, as in the other examples, found myself at the very same moment already falling out of that desire and wishing I were back in it.[10]

While Warnie had been sent to school in England as far back as 1905, Jack was still at home taking lessons from his governess and his mother. Indeed, he knew both Greek and Latin by the age of six. Then, in the winter of 1908, Flora began to feel ill. She was operated on at home shortly afterwards and the younger son was never to forget how after the operation his father, in tears, came into the boy's room and tried to convey the news that his mother had cancer. Warnie was called home from England and like "two frightened urchins" they "huddled for warmth in a bleak world."[11] Their mother, who before had set the even temper of the family, was gradually drawn from them. Before her death on August 23, 1908, she presented each of her sons with a Bible.

Lewis wrote later, "With my mother's death all settled happiness, all that was tranquil and reliable, disappeared from my life. There was to be much fun, many pleasures, many stabs of Joy; but no more of the old security. It was sea and islands now; the great continent had sunk like Atlantis."[12]

The Reverend Thomas Robert Hamilton

Although Albert Lewis's intentions were good, bad advice from the start meant that Lewis's early school-life was disastrous. And although everything showed Jack to be bright, he nevertheless hated all the schools he was forced to attend. First, he was sent, like Warnie before him, to Wynyard School in Watford, Hertfordshire, which when Lewis was there in 1908 consisted of a pair of semi-detached houses with outdoor lavatories and was fast sliding into irreversible squalor. It was described as being "at once brutalising and intellectually stupefying" to Lewis and the other half-dozen unfortunates who suffered from a crazed headmaster who wielded the cane at the slightest provocation.

But after two years he won his freedom. The school collapsed, and the headmaster Robert Capron was certified insane. Years later, when Walter Hooper was living in Lewis's Oxford home as his private secretary, Lewis told him that the blanket on his bed was the same that he had shivered under in that curtainless dormitory at Wynyard.

Warnie *(far left)* and Jack *(in white)* with their mother at
Dundela Villas, 1901

There was, however, one good effect to come out of this debacle. The boys were sent regularly to the nearby church of St. John's, still a fine bastion of Anglo-Catholicism, and it was at this time that Lewis first became an effective believer. "As far as I know," he was to write later, "the instrument was the church to which we were taken twice every Sunday . . . I here heard the doctrines of Christianity . . . taught by men who obviously believed them. As I had no scepticism, the effect was to bring to life what I would already have said that I believed. In this experience there was a great deal of fear . . . I feared for my soul; especially on certain blazing moonlit nights in that curtainless dormitory—how the sound of other boys breathing in their sleep comes back! The effect, so far as I can judge, was entirely good."[13]

But the good he received from St. John's was not entirely apparent to him at the time. There was the bigotry towards Roman Catholics which he had picked up, not from his parents, but from others in his native Ulster. He wrote in the diary he began at Wynyard in November 1909: "We were obliged to go to St. Johns; a church which wanted to be Roman Catholic, but was afraid to say so. A kind of Church abhorred by respectful Irish protestants. Here Wyn Capron, the son of our head master, preached a sermon, better than his usual ones. In this abominable place, of Romish hypocrites, and English liars, the people cross themselves, bow to the Lord's table (which they have the vanity to call an 'altar'), and pray to the Virgin."[14]

Without the mediating influence of their mother at home, things were not going too well. Their father, in his attempts to be closer to the boys, only succeeded in stifling the understanding they had once had. So much so that when Lewis later had spent more time in England the gulf between father and son was every bit as wide as the Irish Sea.

You will have grasped that my father was no fool . . . At the same time he had . . . more power of confusing an issue or taking up a fact wrongly than any man I have ever known . . . The first and simplest barrier to communication was that having earnestly asked, he did not "stay for an answer" or forgot it the moment it was uttered . . . But this was the simplest barrier. Far more often he retained something but something very unlike what you had said . . .

Tell him that a boy called Churchwood had caught a fieldmouse and kept it as a pet and a year or ten years later, he would ask you, "Did you ever hear what became of poor Chickweed who was afraid of the rats?" For his own version, once adopted, was indelible, and attempts to correct it only produced an incredulous "Hm! Well that's not the story you *used* to tell." Sometimes, indeed, he took in the facts you had stated; but truth fared none the better for that. What are facts without interpretation? It was axiomatic to my father . . . that nothing was said or done from an obvious motive. Hence he who in his real life was the most honourable and impulsive of men, and the easiest victim that any knave or imposter could hope to meet, became a positive Machiavel when he knitted his brows and applied to the behaviour of people he had never seen the spectral and labyrinthine operation which he called "reading between the lines." Once embarked upon that, he might make his landfall anywhere in the wide world: and always with unshakable conviction. "I see it all"—"I understand it perfectly"—"It's as plain as a pikestaff" he would say . . .

And besides all these confusions there were the sheer *non sequiturs* when the ground seemed to open at one's feet . . . A certain church in Belfast has both a Greek inscription over the door and a curious tower. "That church is a great landmark," said I, "I can pick it out from all sorts of places—even from the top of Cave Hill." "Such nonsense," said my father, "how could you make out Greek letters three or four miles away?"

One conversation, held several years later, may be recorded as a specimen of these continual cross-purposes. My brother had been speaking of a re-union dinner for the officers of the Nth Division which he had lately attended. "I suppose your friend Collins was there," said my father.

> B. Collins? Oh no. He wasn't in the Nth, you know.
>
> F. (After a pause.) Did these fellows not like Collins then?
>
> B. I don't quite understand. What fellows?
>
> F. The Johnnies that got up the dinner.
>
> B. Oh no, not at all. It was nothing to do with liking or not liking. You see, it was a purely Divisional affair. There'd be no question of asking anyone who hadn't been in the Nth.
>
> F. (After a long pause.) Hm! Well, I'm sure poor Collins was very much hurt.[15]

The boys were not totally without friends and relatives and indeed were always welcome at Glenmachan House, the home of Sir William Quartus Ewart and his wife, their mother's cousin, Lady Ewart. Sir

Little Lea, 1905

Entrance Hall of Little Lea

The author on staircase in
Little Lea

William was a wealthy industrialist and the impressive house became for Jack and Warnie a second home of attics, indoor silences, and endless bookshelves. They roamed there as they liked, and in comparison to Little Lea, life glided like a barge while their real home now bumped like a cart. The boys grew especially fond of the three daughters, Hope, Kelso, and Gundreda. Jack for the rest of his life thought the youngest of them, Gundreda, the most beautiful woman he ever saw. There were the two brothers as well, Robert and Gordon.

Before the collapse of Wynyard, Warnie, being old enough, was sent onto Malvern College. But for Jack it was to Belfast and Campbell College, not a mile from Glenmachan House. This was 1910, and he might have liked it more than he did had it not seemed to him as a boarder "very like living permanently in a large railway station."[16]

A little later he was sent to Cherbourg School, perched high upon the beautiful Malvern Hills over-looking Malvern College. It's much the same in appearance now as it was in 1911 when Lewis was there, and for two years his education began in earnest under the kind and sensible guidance of the headmaster, Arthur C. Allen.

When the boy's father heard of his quite extraordinary success in Latin and Greek he wrote to him on October 27, 1912, saying, "Strange

The author in "the little end room" of Little Lea

Water colour drawing of the little master, by
C. S. Lewis, rediscovered 1920, with the preceding.

1907-8 (?)

Lewis's drawing of the
frog Lord Big

to say I dreamt one night last week of a brilliant star falling through the sky. I suppose I must have been thinking of you when I fell asleep. I certainly woke up with a start thinking of you. Not that you are a 'brilliant star falling thro' the sky.' But perhaps that is the dream message of coming success."[17]

Meanwhile, terrible harm was coming to the lad from an unexpected quarter—the school matron, Miss G. E. Cowie. Well-intentioned though she was, her floundering in the mazes of theosophy, Rosicrucianism, and spiritualism smothered the truth of Christian revelation and left the boy a self-confessed atheist—a rejoicing pagan.

But Lewis persevered as a scholar and at the end of summer term 1913 he won a classical scholarship to Malvern College. Allowed to name his own prize, he was given a copy of Ronald A. MacKenzie's *Teutonic Myth and Legend*. For it was clear now that the vast, cool northernness in Norse mythology was his greatest literary love. Not long afterwards he was to write eight hundred lines of a poem, *Loki Bound*, a pagan tragedy which bewailed the burden of existence imposed on pathetic mankind by the god Odin. And for the moment this thirst for uncluttered legend was assuaged only by the reading of everything he saw having anything to do with it. What had as much as anything mediated the return of Joy—the renaissance of the old bitter-sweet— had been a chance discovery made at Cherbourg School.

"I can lay my hand on the very moment; there is hardly any fact I know so well . . . Someone must have left in the schoolroom a literary periodical: *The Bookman* . . . My eye fell upon a headline and a picture

Wynyard School

Believed to be the schoolroom of Wynyard School

carelessly, expecting nothing. A moment later, as the poet says, 'The sky had turned round.' What I had read were the words *Siegfried and the Twilight of the Gods*. What I had seen was one of Arthur Rackham's illustrations to that volume. . . . Pure 'Northernness' engulfed me: a vision of huge, clear spaces hanging above the Atlantic in the endless twilight of Northern summer, remoteness, severity . . . and almost at the same moment I knew that I had met this before, long, long ago . . . in *Tegner's Drapa*, that Siegfried . . . belonged to the same world as Balder and the sunward-sailing cranes. And with that plunge back into my own past there arose at once, almost like heartbreak, the memory of Joy itself, the knowledge that I had once had what I had now lacked for years, that I was returning at last from exile and desert lands to my own country; and the distance of the Twilight of the Gods and the distance of my own past Joy, both unattainable, flowed together into a single, unendurable sense of desire and loss . . . And at once I knew . . . that to 'have it again' was the supreme and only important object of desire."[18]

"Joy," said Lewis, "is an unsatisfied desire which is itself more desirable than any other satisfaction. I call it Joy, which is here a technical term and must be sharply distinguished both from Happiness and from Pleasure. Joy (in my sense) has indeed one characteristic, and one

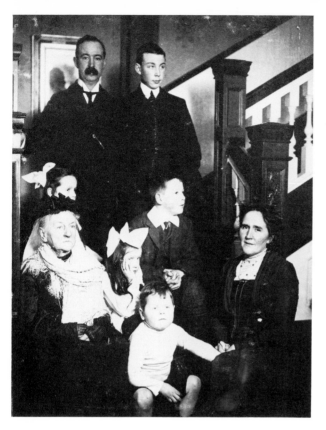

Christmas Day party, 1909. *Left to right: standing,* Albert and Warnie; *seated,* Ruth Hamilton, Jack, Mrs. Mary Warren Hamilton (grandmother of CSL), Harley and John Hamilton, and Mrs. Annie Hamilton

Warnie, Albert Lewis, and Jack, 1910

A tennis party at Glenmachan House, 1910. *Left to right:*
seated, unknown, unknown, unknown, Lily Greeves (sister to
Arthur), Robert Heard Ewart; *standing,* Arthur Greeves,
Gordon Ewart, Jack Lewis

only, in common with them; the fact that anyone who has experienced
it will want it again. Apart from that, and considered only in its quality,
it might almost equally well be called a particular kind of unhappiness
or grief. But then it is a kind we want. I doubt whether anyone who has
tasted it would ever, if both were in his power, exchange it for all the
pleasures in the world. But then Joy is never in our power and pleasure
often is.''[19]

Malvern College overlooks the whole of Worcestershire and beyond. Lewis arrived there in September 1913, and if he had been the
only pupil he would have found the library and some of the masters all
he could have wanted. But he detested the games, the ''preparation for
public life,'' the absorbing preoccupation of most of the boys to achieve
a place in the school's inner ring, and the fagging—the system by
which, without breaking any rules, the older boys could tyrannise the

younger ones. At times exhausted, Lewis pleaded with his father for the whole of the year he was there to have him removed. Until that could take place, however, if it ever would, he clung to the only life-raft he knew, literature, especially mythology. School organisation brought only deeply felt melancholy and for solace he retreated into a "many-islanded sea of poetry and myth."[20]

Later, though, some reminiscence did bring enjoyment and he recalled that the sanitary arrangements were not altogether what one would nowadays expect: "At Malvern all the lavatories were connected

Jack, Warnie, Albert Lewis, and William Hugh Patterson near Little Lea, December 26, 1910

by a channel of water running underneath. It sloped downhill a little and people used to roll up a vast quantity of bumf in the top one, shove it down, and set fire to it. Then there'd be a fireship passing over everybody's bottom all the way down."[21]

While his father had received no unflattering reports of these schools from the elder, more gregarious son, Warnie, he was now convinced that the younger boy's pessimism was not feigned. The schools were causing him considerable damage and something had to be done.

Jack and Warnie on each side
of their father, 1911

Campbell College, Belfast

Cherbourg School

During the Easter vacation of 1914 he wrote to William T. Kirkpatrick, who had been his headmaster at Lurgan College, and asked him to tutor Jack. Kirkpatrick, then sixty-six and living in the rural quiet of Surrey, was taking one or two boarding pupils, and as he had already prepared Warnie for Sandhurst, he consented to cram Jack for Oxford. The one condition he insisted on was that Jack return to Malvern for one final term, and come to him in the autumn of 1914. "If you want to know how I felt," Lewis was to say about this decision, "imagine your own feelings on waking one morning to find that income tax or unrequited love had somehow vanished from the world."[22]

But this wasn't the only pleasant thing of that Easter vacation and it happened in a house close to Little Lea called "Bernagh." While at home Lewis wondered whether he should walk across the road and meet a chap who had long wanted to become his friend, Arthur Greeves. Their families were friends, Arthur was ill, and a message had been sent

The boys and staff of Cherbourg School, c. 1911. *Left to right: middle row,* the lady in white is possibly Miss Cowie; the other adults are Mr. and Mrs. Arthur C. Allen, and Jack is on Mr. Allen's left.

Cherbourg School theatrical, c. 1911. *Left to right: back,*
Clutterbuck, Nadin; *front,* Jack Lewis, Maxwell, Bowen

to say that he would welcome a visit. Jack rarely accepted such a summons, everyone in the house knew that, but with the end of his schooldays in sight his day-to-day melancholy was for once lifted and he accepted. One ponders: this meeting could easily have never taken place and a life-long friendship would never have been realised.

"I found Arthur sitting up in bed," he was to recall. "On the table beside him lay a copy of *Myths of the Norsemen.*

" 'Do *you* like that?' said I.

" 'Do *you* like that?' said he.

"Next moment the book was in our hands, our heads were bent close together, we were pointing, quoting, talking—soon almost shouting—discovering in a torrent of questions that we liked not only the same thing, but the same parts of it and in the same way; that both knew the stab of Joy and that, for both, the arrow was shot from the North. Many thousands of people have had the experience of finding the first friend and it is none the less a wonder; as great a wonder . . . as first

Gundreda Ewart

Glenmachan House

Malvern College

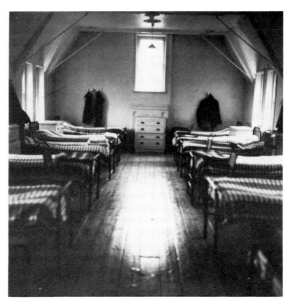

Jack's dormitory at
Malvern College

Bernagh, the home of
Arthur Greeves, across
the road from Little Lea

love, or even a greater. I had been so far from thinking such a friend
possible that I had never even longed for one; no more than I had longed
to be King of England . . . Nothing, I suspect, is more astonishing in any
man's life than the discovery that there do exist people very, very like
himself."[23]

Lewis had every reason to feel happy and excited about this new
friendship, for now his visits home became for the first time a pleasure
rather than a chore. And yet the two were very different; Greeves an
inarticulate Christian and Lewis the high-flown pagan. Lewis was later

Arthur Greeves

One of Arthur Greeves's paintings

Mr. and Mrs. W. T. Kirkpatrick in
front of their home in Little Bookham,
October 10, 1920

The 200-year-old barn
which is all that remains
of the Kirkpatrick home

to say of his friend, "I learned charity from him and failed, for all my efforts, to teach him arrogance in return."[24]

And so he came to the house of William T. Kirkpatrick in the Surrey village of Little Bookham, arriving there on September 19, 1914. The house which is gone now was called "Gastons," but the two-hundred-year-old barn stands yet and the surrounding village and fields are as pleasant as ever. It was here that Lewis's intellect was rescued from what might have been gradual dissipation and for the rest of his life he was grateful for it. And thus he wrote of his tutor:

If ever a man came near to being a purely logical entity, that man was Kirk . . . The idea that human beings should exercise their vocal organs for any purpose except that of communicating or discovering truth was to him preposterous. The most casual remark was taken as a summons to disputation. I soon came to know the differing values of his three openings. The loud cry of "Stop!" was flung in to arrest a torrent of verbiage which could not be endured a moment longer; not because it fretted his patience (he never thought of that)

Afternoon tea at Bernagh, summer 1913. *Left to right:* Tom Greeves, William Greeves, Albert Lewis, Joseph Greeves (Arthur's father), unknown, unknown, unknown, Mrs. Joseph Greeves, and Lily Greeves

but because it was wasting time, darkening counsel. The hastier and quieter "Excuse!" . . . ushered in a correction or distinction merely parenthetical and betokened that, thus set right, your remark might still, without absurdity, be allowed to reach completion. The most encouraging of all was, "I hear you." This meant that your remark was significant and only required refutation; it had risen to the dignity of error. Refutation (when we got so far) always followed the same lines. Had I read this? Had I studied that? Had I any statistical evidence? Had I any evidence in my own experience? And so to the almost inevitable conclusion, "Do you not see then that you had no right etc."

Some boys would not have liked it; to me it was red beef and strong beer . . . Here was talk that was really about something. Here was a man who thought not about you but about what you said. No doubt I snorted and bridled a little at some of my tossings; but, taking it all in all, I loved the treatment. After being knocked down sufficiently often I began to know a few guards and blows, and to put on intellectual muscle. In the end, unless I flatter myself, I became a not contemptible sparring partner. It was a great day when the man who had so long been engaged in exposing my vagueness at last cautioned me against the dangers of excessive subtlety.[25]

But the respect flowed mutually between them, and of Lewis, Kirkpatrick—not a man to bandy compliments with a pupil—said in a letter to Albert Lewis on September 16, 1915, that Clive was the finest translator of Greek plays he had ever met. Warnie, who had also been through Little Bookham on his way to Sandhurst, wrote of his brother at this time: "For Jack these days were paradisal without qualification, his letters of the time being charged with the intoxication of literary discovery."[26]

And so to Oxford.

PART II
Oxford

The fabled spires of Oxford

It is well that there are palaces of peace
And discipline and dreaming and desire,
Lest we forget our heritage and cease
The Spirit's work—to hunger and aspire:

Lest we forget that we were born divine,
Now tangled in red battle's animal net,
Murder the work and lust the anodyne,
Pains of the beast 'gainst bestial solace set.

But this shall never be: to us remains
One city that has nothing of the beast,
That was not built for gross, material gains,
Sharp, wolfish power or empire's glutted feast.

We are not wholly brute. To us remains
A clean, sweet city lulled by ancient streams,
A place of vision and of loosening chains,
A refuse of the elect, a tower of dreams.

She was not builded out of common stone
But out of all men's yearning and all prayer
That she might live, eternally our own,
The Spirit's stronghold—barred against despair.

C. S. Lewis, *Spirits in Bondage*

Lewis was now a scholar of University College, founded in 1249 and the oldest of the twenty fully recognised colleges that then made up the

University College, Oxford

University of Oxford. When he arrived on April 26, 1917, the scout or college servant showed him up to a magnificent set of rooms in the first quadrangle. They turned out, however, to belong to "a tremendous blood" then fighting "at the front"[1] and so it was with some reluctance that Lewis had to move into a more modest affair, Staircase XII, Room 5, in the adjoining Radcliffe Quad.

These are the rooms he was to occupy for his entire residence at University College, or "Univ." as it is known in Oxford. The college

The front quad of
University College

CSL *(standing on the right)* with the only other members of
"Univ." in the college photograph of 1917

buildings have changed very little since then. In fact the view from his sitting-room window is exactly the same, and one which Lewis enjoyed especially. He wrote in a letter to Arthur Greeves, "It is getting to be quite homely to me this room, especially when I come back to it by firelight and find the kettle boiling. How I love kettles!"[2]

But it has to be remembered that this, sadly, was Oxford in war-time. In fact there were only twelve men in Univ. at the time, of which eight and the dean appear in the official college photograph of that year. There were still chaps swimming *au naturel* in that little "gentlemen—only" backwater of the Cherwell called "Parson's Pleasure"; still a few punts on the river. But, on the whole, things were greatly changed.

"Last night," he wrote to his friend Greeves, "at about nine o'clock I wandered out into the deserted quad. & after 'strolling' for some time went up a staircase where nobody goes in these war days into the oldest part of the College. The windows here are all tiny ivy covered & stained so that it was very dark already. I walked up & down long passages, with locked rooms on each side, revelling in 'desolation.' The 'oaks' of these rooms were mostly (as I say) locked, but by good luck I found one open & went in. On the inner door the faded name 'Mr. Carter' greeted

Parson's Pleasure

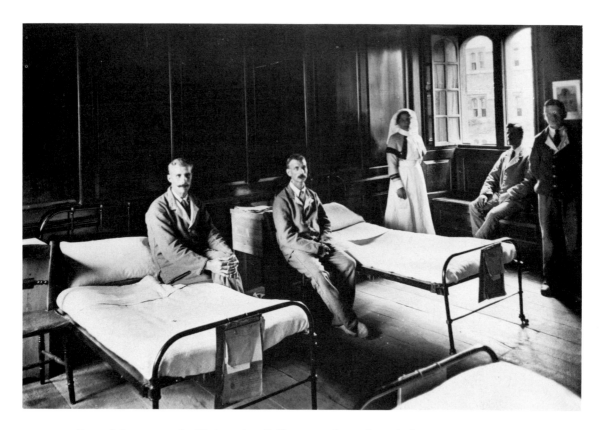

One of the rooms in University College used as a hospital
during World War I

me: inside was a tiny room, smaller than my own at home, very dark &
thick with dust. It seemed almost sacrilege to turn on the lights in such
a forsaken place, but I simply had to inspect it. The furniture was all
just as the owner must have left it & his photos were there on the wall.
I also inspected his books (mostly ordinary Everymen) including
Lavengro, *Tristram Shandy*, Burke's *Speeches* & *Tom Jones*. I suppose
this sounds trivial to you; but perhaps you can picture the strange
poetry of the thing in such a time and place. I wonder who Carter is,
and if he has been killed yet, & why he left his pile of music so untidily
on the dressing table?

   "I had another thrill too, when I got up (quite dark by now) into a
sort of attic place full of old trunks etc. & heard a strange thumping
noise just beside me. I was mystified for a while, till I realised that I was
just behind the big college clock & this was the ticking of it. You know
how sad and grand a big clock sounds in a lonely place."[3]

   Yes indeed, there is a strange poetry. Arthur Norwood Carter,
whose rooms Lewis was in that night, matriculated as a Rhodes Scholar

The smoking room at the
Oxford Union

The "Schools" building being used as a hospital during World War I

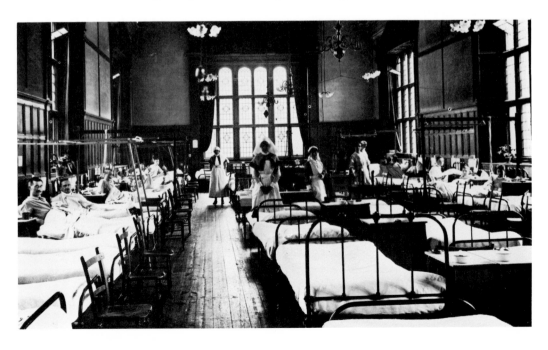

The home of Mrs. Janie King Moore, 56 Ravenswood Road, Bristol

"Hillsboro House," where CSL lived with the Moores from 1923 to 1930

A group of Keble O.T.C. Cadets, 1917. (Lewis is looking over
"Paddy" Moore's left shoulder.)

from New Brunswick in 1913. He not only survived the war, but has
sent two sons, also Rhodes Scholars, to Univ.

Determined atheist though he was at this time, never in his life was
Lewis a man to live a lie, and whilst he took a scholarship in the
foremost English university, he now felt duty bound also to take his
place in her armed forces. He didn't have to sign up. His father implored
him not to do so. As an Irish subject Lewis could quite easily have
gained exemption. But in this he just felt duty bound.

And so in June of 1917 he moved across the University from Univ.
to be billeted in Keble College with the Officers' Training Corps. By
alphabetical accident he shared a room with E. F. C. "Paddy" Moore.
Paddy's home was in Bristol, and his mother and sister came down and
took temporary lodgings in Oxford to be near him. Lewis met them that
very week and thereafter they were to see one another frequently. This
chance meeting was to have great effect on the rest of Lewis's life.

The young men grew fast friends and two surviving photographs
from those days of tense expectancy show them in one case with their
battalion, and again together punting on the river. But it had to come to

sooner or later, they knew that, and on September 18 they learned that there were just four weeks left before possibly going to the front. And such was Lewis's feeling of contentment with the whole Moore family that he chose to spend three weeks of this in Bristol and only the last few days at home with his father. Albert Lewis was deeply hurt, but the attention which his son had lavished on the Moore family was more extensive than even he knew.

The Moores lived at 56 Ravenswood Road, Bristol, and it was here that Jack and Paddy were to be together for the last time before being shipped to France; Lewis with the 3rd Somerset Light Infantry and Paddy with his Rifle Brigade. Paddy's sister, Maureen—now Lady Dunbar of Hempriggs—was twelve at the time, but she told Walter Hooper years later that she could recall very distinctly hearing Lewis and her brother promise most solemnly that if one or the other of them survived the war the survivor would look after Paddy's mother and Lewis's father.

Suddenly, on Thursday, November 15, they were ordered to the front following a forty-eight-hour leave. As it was impossible for Lewis

Lewis and his friend "Paddy" Moore punting on the Cherwell, summer 1917

to go home, he set out for Mrs. Moore's home in Bristol from whence he sent the following telegram to his father: "Have arrived Bristol on 48 hours leave. Report Southampton Saturday. Can you come Bristol? If so meet at station. Reply Mrs. Moore's address 56 Ravenswood Road, Redlands, Bristol. Jack." Mr. Lewis wired back, "Don't understand telegram. Please write."[4] Clive Lewis did write and on November 16 he wired that he must report to Southampton by four o'clock on the seventeenth. His father made no effort to meet him either in Bristol or in Southampton, and Lewis crossed to France on November 17 without seeing him. He reached the front line on his nineteenth birthday, November 29. Writing about his war-time experience many years later he said:

"Until the great German attack came in the Spring we had a pretty quiet time. Even then they attacked not us but the Canadians on our right, merely 'keeping us quiet' by pouring shells into our line about

Jack with his father on his last visit home before going to war, October 1917

Albert and Jack in the Garden of
Little Lea, July 1919

CSL after returning from the war,
1919

University College freshmen of January 1919. *Back row, left to right:* A. C. Brashaw, C. L. Barwell, J. de F. Thompson, R. E. Owen, A. K. Hamilton-Jenkin, G. O. Vinter, K. S. Sandford, H. L. Addleshaw, T. E. Lindop, H. L. Hopper. *Middle row:* N. S. Millican, P. C. Raiment, G. M. Morton, P. W. Rucker, C. A. Minoprio, K. M. Davie, L. Chalk, O. D. Ballinger, H. P. Mitchell. *Front row:* M. M. Hallett, D. R. Gawler, H. P. Blunt, B. P. Wyllie, G. D. Kirwan, G. Chilton, C. S. Lewis, R. M. S. Pasley, A. R. L. Gaussen, H. W. Turner.

three a minute all day. I think it was that day I noticed how a greater terror overcomes a less: a mouse that I met (and a poor shivering mouse it was, as I was a poor shivering man) made no attempt to run from me. Through the winter, weariness and water were our chief enemies. I have gone to sleep marching and woken again and found myself marching still. One walked in the trenches in thigh gum boots with water above the knee; one remembers the icy stream welling up inside the boot when you punctured it on concealed barbed wire. Familiarity with both the very old and the very recent dead confirmed that view of corpses which had been formed the moment I saw my dead mother. . . . But for the rest, the war—the frights, the cold, the smell of high explosive, the horribly smashed men still moving like half-crushed beetles, the sitting or standing corpses, the landscape of sheer earth without a blade of grass, the boots worn day and night till they seemed to grow to your feet—all this shows rarely and faintly in memory. . . . One imaginative moment seems now to matter more than the realities that followed. It

Jack in "the little end room" of Little Lea on his return from the war, December 1919

Albert Lewis in his study, May 25, 1920

The original kilns

A wardrobe in The Kilns carved
by CSL's grandfather
Richard Lewis

Proctor's Rostra, Sheldonian Theater, from which Lewis would have read the essay that won him the Chancellor's English Essay Prize in 1921

A caricature of Albert Lewis which appeared in a Belfast newspaper, 1921, celebrating his impressive use of the English language was the first bullet I heard—so far from me that it 'whined' like a journalist's or a peacetime poet's bullet. At that moment there was something not exactly like fear, much less like indifference: a little quavering signal that said, 'This is War. This is what Homer wrote about.' "[5]

Lewis didn't find out until later that his friend Paddy was killed in March 1918, and indeed the war for Lewis was not to last much longer. He captured a small company of Germans single-handed, which experience he told Walter Hooper was more accident than angry aggression —"They weren't really afraid of me, but just walked out with their hands up." He was wounded on Mount Bernenchon during the Battle of Arras on April 15, 1918, from an English shell which burst behind him. Hence the greetings of an aunt who said with obvious relief "Oh! So *that's* why you were wounded in the back!"

He was now to see a number of cluttered military hospitals. However, ever since his arrival back in England on May 25, 1918, he had begun compiling *Spirits in Bondage,* under the pseudonym Clive Hamilton, a volume of poems which he hoped would be his first steps towards poetic fame. With it being his first publication, the proud son sent a copy to his father. But Albert Lewis wasn't deceived into thinking that literary cleverness justified heresy. He returned it to Jack, saying, "I shouldn't leave this about. The servants might see it!"[6] But still for Lewis, more than for many others, Lord Byron's words "I will cut myself a path through this world or perish in the attempt. I will achieve grandeur but never with dishonour" were despairingly true.[7] Indeed it

A group of cousins at Glenmachan House, 1920. *Left to right: standing,* Gordon Ewart, Robert Ewart; *seated,* Anne McCreedy, Albert Lewis, Cherry Robbins

The Divinity School, Bodleian Library

was on this that his atheism thrived so vehemently, and what a formidable pagan he was.

Lewis had always been reluctant in defining his religious beliefs, but once, when pushed very hard by Arthur Greeves, he wrote to him on October 12, 1916, saying: "You know, I think, that I believe in no religion. There is absolutely no proof for any of them, and from a philosophical standpoint Christianity is not even the best. All religions, that is, all mythologies to give them their proper name are merely man's own invention—Christ as much as Loki. Primitive man found himself surrounded by all sorts of terrible things he didn't understand . . . Thus religion, that is to say mythology grew up. Often, too, great men were regarded as gods after their death—such as Heracles or Odin: thus after the death of a Hebrew philosopher Yeshua (whose name we have corrupted into Jesus) he became regarded as a god, a cult sprang up, which was afterwards connected with the ancient Hebrew Jahweh-worship, and so Christianity came into being—one mythology among many . . .

The Duke Humfrey Library

Illuminated manuscript in the Duke Humfrey Library

Magdalen College Tower

Of course, mind you, I am not laying down as a certainty that there *is* nothing outside the material world . . . this would be foolish."[8]

And so back to the dreaming spires. He came up to Oxford in January 1919 and within two months was already a published poet. He was determined that there be no flirtations with the idea of the supernatural. All the images he associated with Joy were, he concluded, sheer fantasies. He had at last "seen through" them. The important thing was to get ahead with the "good life"—and where was it better with the University returning to normal? Well, Lewis's confusions at the time must be taken for what they were, but at least now with the war over, his undergraduate days began in earnest; and with them his pledged responsibility for Mrs. Moore and Maureen.

After fulfilling two more terms of statutory residence in Univ., he decided to take rented accommodations with the Moores in Headington, to the east of the University. And this saw the beginning of many unsettling years of domestic drudgery and worry. Not only was the allowance from his father not sufficient for a man in a house with two total dependents, but it brought unnecessary frustration at a time when

The Fellows of Magdalen College in 1928. The Fellows on page 60 are, *standing, left to right:* G. R. S. Snow, Professor E. C. Titchmarsh, H. C. Stewart (organist), R. Segar, K. B. McFarlane, E. Hope, ?, S. G. Lee, H. M. D. Parker; *sitting, left to right:* Professor C. C. Foligno, J. M. Thompson, Sir Charles Sherrington, Professor W. H. Perkin, Reverend A. W. Chute, Reverend C. R. Carter, E. S. Craig.

his studies demanded his undivided attention. In fact it wasn't for many years, after repeated flitting and arguments with landladies, that they bought and settled into their own house, The Kilns, with its pond and woodlands in the village of Headington Quarry.

This new "family" though, which Jack had seemingly acquired almost to the exclusion of his own, was, not surprisingly, a source of great worry to his father. Warnie also was anxious over the lack of attention Albert Lewis was receiving from his other son. The father wrote to Warren on May 20, 1919, saying, "I confess I do not know what to do or say about Jack's affair. It worries and depresses me greatly. All I know about the lady is that she is old enough to be his mother—that she is separated from her husband and that she is in poor circumstances. I also know that Jack has drawn cheques in her favour running up to £10—for what I don't know. If Jacks were not an impetuous, kind hearted creature who could be cajoled by any woman who has been through the mill, I should not be so uneasy. Then there is the husband whom I have always been told is a scoundrel, but the absent are always to blame . . ."[9] And again, writing to Warren on June 25, 1919, he said,

The Fellows on page 61 are, *standing, left to right:* R. P. Longden, ?, C. S. Lewis, C. E. Brownrigg (Headmaster of Magdalen College School), C. T. Onions, J. T. Christie, ?, M. H. MacKeith, G. R. Driver, J. J. Manley, Reverend H. E. Salter; *sitting, left to right:* Sir Herbert Warren (President of Magdalen), Professor C. H. Turner, P. V. M. Benecke, Reverend F. E. Brightman, Professor J. A. Smith, Professor H. L. Bowman, Professor A. L. Dixon, Professor A. G. Tansley.

CSL in his rooms at
Magdalen College, Oxford,
November 25, 1950

"Come in!" CSL in his College rooms, as he would have been
seen by his pupils, November 25, 1950

CSL in his College rooms, November 25, 1950

"I am afraid I understand the situation too well. He has never once since he went to Oxford come straight home to me when he got leave. Always Mrs. Moore first."[10]

Indeed, it seems that Lewis had a deal of youthful infatuation for Mrs. Moore, who was already forty-five when they first met. Her husband, Courtenay Edward Moore (1870–1951) left her and the two children when Maureen was still a young child and the "Beast," as Mrs. Moore called him, never saw his family again.

In this relationship Lewis the pagan was at his height. Mrs. Moore tried to follow him everywhere, and when separated they exchanged daily letters. The result was the greatest rift that the Lewis family was to experience. Although father and son still corresponded, Mrs. Moore was never discussed and for many years hence Jack was to regard the semi-annual visits home as a chore.

"On the other hand," his brother was to write many years later, "it would be wildly misleading to suggest that my brother lived the life of a solitary and embittered recluse. The case was quite otherwise. As all his friends will bear witness, he was a man with an outstanding gift for pastime with good company, for laughter and the love of friends—a gift which found full scope in any number of holidays and walking tours, the joyous character of his response to these being well conveyed in his letters. He had, indeed, a remarkable talent for friendship, particularly for friendship of an uproarious kind, masculine and argumentative but never quarrelsome."[11] What did Dr. Samuel Johnson say about it? "The size of a man's understanding might be justly measured by his mirth."[12]

Lewis's academic work prospered, though, and much of it was done in the Bodleian Library. The "Bod" is constructed around a central "Schools Quad" of which the Divinity School was finished first, in 1480, and was thought by Lewis to be the most beautiful room he had

CSL, Maureen, and Mrs. Moore at Perranporth, Cornwall, August 1927. The dog is "Baron Papworth."

ever seen. Above it and constructed at the same time, to serve as the sole University library, is the Duke Humfrey, founded on the benefaction of the same Duke Humfrey of Gloucester and still holds his entire personal library. That side, in fact, took fourteen years to complete for halfway through, the King, Henry VIII, dragged away his builders to work on the chapel at Eton. The rest of the quad was due to an endowment by Sir Thomas Bodley, a member of Queen Elizabeth's diplomatic service and a proctor of the University, and was finished with an effigy of the new monarch James I flatteringly adorned by Religion and Fame.

Writing to his father about it, Lewis said: "I spend all my mornings in the Bodleian . . . If only you could smoke, and if only there were

"The Trout," a 14th-century pub, Godstow, Oxford, of which CSL was especially fond

upholstered chairs, the Bodleian would be one of the most delightful places in the world. I sit in 'Duke Humphrey's Library,' the oldest part, a Fifteenth Century building with a very beautiful painted wooden ceiling above me and a little mullioned window on my left hand through which I look down on the garden of Exeter where, these mornings, I see the sudden squalls of wind and rain driving the first blossoms off the fruit trees and snowing the lawn with them ... The library itself—I mean the books—is mostly in a labyrinth of cellars under the neighbouring squares. This room however is full of books ... which stand in little cases at right angles to the wall, so that between each pair there is

Owen Barfield, CSL, Cecil and Daphne Harwood, Sussex, c. 1930

A walking tour in Wales, c. 1935. *Left to right:* Cecil Harwood,
CSL, Walter O. Field, Eric Beckett, Alan Hanbury-Sparrow,
and Owen Barfield (who was taking the picture)

a kind of little 'box' . . . and in these boxes one sits and reads . . . There
is not, as in modern libraries, a forbidding framed notice to shriek
'Silence': on the contrary the more moderate request 'Talk little and
tread lightly.' There is indeed always a faint murmur going on of semi-
whispered conversation in neighbouring boxes. It disturbs no one. I
rather like to hear the hum of the hive."[13]

In another letter to his father, on February 4, 1919, he said, "Much
to my surprise I have had 'greatness thrust upon me.' There is a literary
club in College called the Martlets, limited to 12 undergraduate members: it is over three hundred years old, and alone of all College Clubs

has its minutes preserved in the Bodleian. I have been elected Secretary
... and so if I am forgotten of all else, at least a specimen of my hand-
writing will be preserved to posterity."[14]

In fact the antiquity of the club was just a legend, for it was formed
in 1892 and was a society largely devoted to literature, with carefully
kept minute books. Mind, when it appeared that the minutes were not
being kept as carefully as they should be, members complained. At the
thirty-sixth meeting in 1900 "The Minutes of the last meeting were read
and carried after their scantiness and baldness had been commented on
—qualities undesirable in Minutes, which the Secretary strove to excuse on account of the melancholy that had overfallen him as the end
of his University career drew nigh."[15] Occasionally a member had to be
jogged out of his indolence. Such seems to have been the case at the
fifty-third meeting in 1902: "It was decided that Mr. Tomlinson should
write a paper, or get Mr. Peile to write a paper, or should be expelled
from the Martlets. Mr. Tomlinson hummed, hawed, stammered, stut-
tered, protested, expostulated, cried, screamed, shouted aloud. But the
Society was adamant towards Mr. Tomlinson."[16]

Albert Lewis at Bangor, County
Down, 1928

Hardly need Lewis have worried about posterity. Below the Duke Humfrey is the largest collection of Lewis papers in the world.

But the Martlets did more than read papers. They dined too—always their literary interests being emphasised in the menu. On the occasion of their hundredth meeting in 1906 they had

> *Consommé Mermaid*
> *Sauce Walter Scott*
> *Suprême de smale Foweles*
> *Mouton rôti à la C Lamb*
> *Chartreuse à la Martlets*
> *Diablotines à la Milord Byron* [17]

Dinners such as the Martlets enjoyed are not a delight of yesteryear. Traditions linger long in the University and nowhere are they more strongly upheld than in the college dining clubs. After the seven courses or more, the members retire to another room for dessert—port, choice fruits as to the season, and talk, long into the night such as Lewis sampled.

Unlike many establishments, at Oxford a man's career is assessed in just several days of continuous and rigorous examination. This ordeal is carried on in the dreaded "Schools." But like many things in this university even the coldest of tasks is warmed by long-held tradition, and the Statutes still require full academic dress, or "subfusc," to be worn on all public occasions including examinations. And when it's all over, part of that same tradition requires a man's friends to gather

Jack, Mrs. Moore, and Warnie at The Kilns, 1930

Dovedale, Derbyshire

"The Bull i' th' Thorn" at
Hurdlow, Derbyshire

The author and Owen Barfield
taking tea in "The Bull i' th'
Thorn," Derbyshire

with champagne and celebrate his final escape, although with Lewis and his contemporaries beer would have been more traditional.

Lewis was to sample this treatment several times, for after taking a double First in Greats (that is, Classics and Philosophy) he set his sights on a college Fellowship and took a brilliant First in English just the very next year in 1923.

Still, despite his triple Firsts a Fellowship in one of the colleges eluded him. There was talk of going to another university. That he might become a schoolmaster was suggested—but his inability to play games might count against him. Others, however, urged him to be patient, and he stayed in Oxford considering himself a candidate for a Fellowship in Philosophy. Then his fortune changed. His old philosophy tutor, E. F. Carritt, took a year to teach in the United States and Lewis was asked to deputise. At this time Lewis attended meetings of the Oxford Philosophical Society and, despite his love for English Literature, he disapproved of English as a final honour school. And yet he tried for anything going. He wrote to his father on November 22, 1923, of his first pupil that year in Univ.:

Owen Barfield and the author on the same walk in Derbyshire as CSL and Barfield took in 1935

Lewis and Maud (Mrs. Owen) Barfield in a barge on the
Thames, London, c. 1930

"I have got recently ONE pupil . . . a youth of eighteen who is
trying to get a Classical Scholarship . . . I fear we shall win no laurels
by him. I questioned him about his classical reading: our dialogue was
something like this:

> Self: 'Well, Sandeman, what Greek authors have you been reading?'
> Sand: (cheerfully) 'I can never remember. Try a few names and I'll see if I
> get on to any.'
> Self: (a little dampened) 'Have you read any Euripides?'
> Sand: 'No.'
> Self: 'Any Sophocles?'
> Sand: 'Oh yes.'
> Self: 'What plays of his have you read?'
> Sand: (after a pause) 'Well—the Alcestis.'
> Self: (apologetically) 'But isn't that by Euripides?'
> Sand: (with the genial surprise of a man who finds £1 where he thought
> there was only a 10/- note) 'Really. Is it now? Then by Jove I HAVE
> read some Euripides.' "[18]

Before the year was out he had applied for several Fellowships but
the only one offered him was a Fellowship in English Language and
Literature at Magdalen College—and he accepted it. He wrote at once
to his father on August 14, 1925, saying: "I am rather glad of the change.

I have come to think that if I had the mind, I have not the brain and nerves for a life of pure philosophy. A continued search among the abstract roots of things, a perpetual questioning of all that plain men take for granted, a chewing the cud for fifty years over inevitable ignorance and a constant frontier watch on the little tidy lighted conventional world of science and daily life—is this the best life for temperaments such as ours? . . . No one sympathises with your adventures in that subject because no one understands them: and if you struck treasure trove no one would be able to use it.''[19]

By 1925 Lewis's financial worries were finally over; for now he was tutoring in his own right, and a full member of the Senior Common Room of Magdalen College. Tutorials still happen in exactly the same way nowadays as they did when Lewis gave them. A chap will come once a week to see his tutor and read an essay. And afterwards there would be talk about the next week's work and perhaps a glass of sherry or a pint of beer. It's said of Lewis that he was sparing of his compliments but quick to notice any excellence of usage—and of his public lectures that he was the most popular speaker in the University, always attracting overflow crowds.

Martin Moynihan, sometime British High Commissioner to Lesotho and an ex-pupil of Lewis's described his tutorials in a toast given to the Stamford Dining Club of Brasenose College on the evening of June 6, 1978: '' 'Come in!' Lewis had a resonant and musical voice. When, having emerged from the Cloisters, crossed the New Buildings lawn, you were admitted to Lewis's lofty, white-bookshelved, high-windowed, Chesterfielded room, you knew something thrilling was about to begin. Or, at times, something the reverse, something flattening, a just rebuke—'You have *dragged* into your essay a quotation from the Gospels. I regard that as a gross blemish!' ''

One of the traditional buses going up Headington Hill, Oxford

While Lewis always argued with seriousness and drew on his vast learning in his tutorials and public lectures, his uproarious sense of humour was always close to the surface. No where was his particular talent for punning more evident than at dinner parties or when entertaining guests at Magdalen's High Table. On one memorable occasion one of the courses was a haggis, the national dish of Scotland, consisting of the blood and guts of sheep. Seated next to Lewis was a Portuguese dignitary who, while eating the haggis, remarked that he felt like a "gastronomic Columbus." "The comparison is wayward in your case," replied Lewis. "Why not a vascular da Gama?"

It would be in his rooms in Magdalen that he would have given his tutorials. And it's there, too, that he entertained his friends Owen Barfield, the lawyer, A. C. Harwood, a schoolmaster, and Professor J. R. R. Tolkien, who with Dr. Robert Havard, Charles Williams, the novelist, Lord David Cecil, Hugo Dyson, Nevill Coghill and his brother, along with others, later formed themselves into the literary group known as the Inklings.

Barfield and Harwood had in fact been elected to scholarships in the University at the same time as Lewis—and they were two of his closest friends. With them he talked, drank beer, smoked pipes, and took long walks in the country.

"My happiest hours," he once said, "are spent with three or four old friends in old clothes tramping together and putting up in small pubs—or else sitting up till the small hours in someone's college rooms talking nonsense, poetry, Theology, metaphysics over beer, tea and pipes. There's no sound I like better than adult male laughter."[20]

But there was sadness at this time too. In the summer of 1929 he received word that his father's health had suddenly begun to fail. On July 25, 1929, he wrote to Arthur Greeves, whose father had died a few years previously, saying: "You will remember from your own experience how horrible one feels when the people whom one ought to love, but doesn't very much, are ill and in need of your help & sympathy; when you have to behave as love would dictate and yet feel all the time as if you were doing nothing—because you can't give what's really wanted. Among other things I have to face the prospect that it may be my duty to get him permanently over here—with God knows what upsets & difficulties for everyone I care about—you, Minto, Warnie, myself, everyone."[21] "Minto" was his nickname for Mrs. Moore.

Albert Lewis was seized with pain on July 20 and entered a nursing home on July 25 for a series of X-rays. Immediately his external examining in Cambridge was over, Lewis set off for home, arriving there on August 13. On August 25 he wrote to Warnie, who was stationed in Shanghai, giving him a full account of their father's illness, the cause of which was believed to be a "narrowing of the passage in one of the bowels."[22] This was to be one of the most exhausting periods of Lewis's life as his father was often in terrible agony; and, being in his own home, the chief share of nursing fell upon Lewis, who was up most nights with his father and served him with touching devotion. They were lonely too for the third member of their family and on August 29 Lewis wrote to his brother, saying, "I would give a pint of blood—nay, what's more a tooth (stipulating for a general anaesthetic) if you would throw a pebble at the window and announce your unexpected return."[23]

In September Albert was removed to hospital and an operation discovered cancer. As the doctors thought Albert might still live for some years, and as Lewis's work for the next term was becoming des-

The croquet lawn that CSL could see from his rooms in Magdalen College

Magdalen College Chapel

perate, the doctors advised him to return to England. He arrived in
Oxford on September 22 only to learn by wire on the morning of September
25 that his father was worse. He caught the train an hour later,
and on arriving in Belfast the next morning, he discovered his father
had died on the afternoon of the twenty-fifth.

Warnie first learned of his father's death from a wire Lewis sent on
September 27, none of the letters about Albert's illness reaching him
till sometime in October. Warnie, having now no home, as it was decided
they would sell Little Lea, both Lewis and Mrs. Moore wrote
urging him to come and live with them in Oxford. Meanwhile, it was
decided to leave Little Lea as it was till Warnie's arrival in England—
which was not until April 16, 1930.

It is perhaps most fitting here to record what Warnie said in the
memoir to his brother's *Letters*. "The three of us were at home together
for the last time in 1927: it is pleasant to record that my father noted
this in his journal as 'a very pleasant holiday—roses all the way.' "[24]

The effect of Albert's death upon Lewis unfolded itself in several
ways. The "discovery," as it were, of his father's goodness and the
recognition of how "shabbily" he had treated him was almost certainly
one of the things which later led him to become a regular penitent in

Magdalen College choir

the church confessional. More immediate, however, was the exchange of his regular walking tours for solitary strolls during which he examined minutely his conscience. In any case, his grief led to self-examination, this to remorse, and so on until he achieved a hitherto unknown quiet of mind.

The walking tours were resumed, and as they cannot all be reconstructed it is as well to jump a little ahead to a particular one. In 1935 Lewis and Barfield took a walking tour of Derbyshire, in many ways their favourite, and one they were not to forget.

Writing about it to Arthur Greeves on April 23, 1935, Lewis said, "I am just back from my walking tour with Barfield . . . this year in Derbyshire . . . It is appreciably more like my ideal country than any I have yet seen. It is limestone mountains: which means, from the practical point of view, that it has the jagg'd sky lines and deep vallies of ordinary mountainous country, but with this important difference, that owing to the paleness of the rock and the extreme clarity of the rivers, it is *light* instead of sombre—sublime yet smiling—like the delectable mountains."[25]

They entered the county from Staffordshire by Rudyard Lake. Then after lunch down the Goyt Valley to Chapel-en-le-Frith and so next day to Kinder Downfall, where the shallow river Kinder plunges off the edge of the peaty moor. Here on windy days when the sun warms the moorside the water is blown into myriad droplets of rainbowed light. Crossing Kinder Scout and down Grindsbrook they came to Edale and at last stopped the night in Castleton. Next day they walked up the Winnat Pass and across Tideswell Moor to Wardlow and Monsal Dale. It's just a short way now to Ashford in the Water and Bakewell and on again the fourth day to Ashbourne and Dovedale. "Was you ever in Dovedale?" wrote Lord Byron to a friend. "I can assure you there are things in Derbyshire as noble as Greece or Switzerland."[26]

On July 27, 1978, Owen Barfield and Walter Hooper took tea in the "Bull i' th' Thorn," a fifteenth-century pub at Hurdlow near Buxton and planned the reconstruction of that memorable walk. It was on this occasion that Barfield recounted that first meeting and his earliest visits to see Lewis:

When we first met in 1919 Jack was living, at least part of the time, in 28 Warneford Road just outside Oxford with Mrs. Moore. Mrs. Moore was a bit of a mystery to us because she didn't appear on the scene. I think he wanted to appear as much as possible as an undergraduate with a room of his own—not connected in a domestic way with anybody. I used to have tea with him and, for some reason, never actually met Mrs. Moore. But it was a little time after that, when I think I went a little more often—probably by that time we were both graduates—and I remember I sometimes went somewhat later in the evening and we would be either reading aloud or possibly talking, in the drawing room it would be. Jack would suddenly say "Excuse me for a few minutes. I've got to go and do Mrs. Moore's 'jars.'" And it was some time before I actually knew what that meant. In fact I don't think I ever rightly asked him, but I discovered a little later that it was his name, possibly a general Irish name, for hot water bottles. He used to go and prepare hot water bottles—evidently more than one as it was plural—for her bed before she retired.

I suppose about that time I, and Harwood who used to go as well, sort of made a plan that we should try and meet this mysterious Mrs. Moore. So you took an opportunity if you met her in the passage or somewhere to get into conversation with her, and before very long it was very much like coming to an ordinary house and meeting a man's family as well as himself. And I can remember many happy times both for myself alone and later when my wife and I were living near Oxford we would go and see them and all be together.

Mrs. Moore wasn't a woman with a great deal of "conversation"; she didn't know very much and wasn't much interested in what was going on in the World—more interested in her own affairs, but a very nice woman and I and my wife liked her very much.

Of course we only saw her when she was entertaining and we didn't know what went on in the house when we weren't there. But when we read the references to her in Warnie's introduction to the *Letters* we were shocked, almost horrified, of the impression it gave of her character. We remembered so well how she had almost *pampered* them it seemed. I remember my wife saying once as we came away, "She almost spoils those boys!"

It is still quiet in Derbyshire, but some years before that walking tour and back in Oxford, things were coming to a head for Lewis. As a man who believed in the essential economy of nature, the existence of Joy as distinct from pleasure had always troubled him. What was it? Where could he place his finger and say "This is it"? He couldn't. Slowly but surely his intellect was being bullied into the corner—and he knew it. He was later to write:

"I was going up Headington Hill on the top of a bus. Without words and (I think) almost without images, a fact about myself was somehow presented to me. I became aware that I was holding something at bay, or shutting something out."[27]

This had been no straight road as to Damascus; more like a school-boy's meanderings home. Yet the destination was the same. An urgent dispatch to Barfield read: "Terrible things are happening to me. The 'Spirit' or 'Real I' is showing an alarming tendency to become much more personal and is taking the offensive and behaving just like *God*. You'd better come on Monday at the latest or I may have entered a monastery."[28] And so, it had happened:

"You must picture me alone in that room in Magdalen, night after night, feeling, whenever my mind lifted even for a second from my work, the steady, unrelenting approach of Him whom I so earnestly desired not to meet. That which I greatly feared had at last come upon me. In the Trinity Term of 1929 I gave in, and admitted that God was God, and knelt and prayed: perhaps, that night, the most dejected and reluctant convert in all England. I did not then see what is now the most shining and obvious thing; the Divine humility which will accept a convert even on such terms. The Prodigal Son at least walked home on his own feet. But who can duly adore that love which will open the high gates to a prodigal who is brought in kicking, struggling, resentful, and darting his eyes in every direction for a chance of escape? The words *compelle intrare*, compel them to come in, have been so abused by wicked men that we shudder at them; but, properly understood, they plumb the depth of the Divine mercy. The hardness of God is kinder than the softness of men, and His compulsion is our liberation."[29]

The cloisters of Magdalen are a quiet part of Oxford, and for Lewis it would have been the same. But people come and go, yet on a warm Trinity evening the quad will still have that sweetness about it and the

Anthony Marchington astride a motorcycle with sidecar of the same vintage as Jack and Warnie drove to Whipsnade Zoo

cloisters will still whisper to the same cool fragrance. But, be that as it may; if there were great rejoicings in Heaven that particular evening as Lewis crossed the quad to begin his now regular chapel attendances, you can be sure that all this would have maintained its usual quiet discretion. The choristers, coming over from their school across the way to sing the Evensong might have had a question or two, though. Who's the new face? What's *he* doing here? We *know* now of course. It was the most reluctant convert in all England about to become perhaps the finest religious thinker of the age.

But he was still only a theist. And it was not until one Saturday evening, September 19, 1931, when Lewis invited Tolkien and Hugo Dyson to dine that the final piece fell into place. The three of them took an after-dinner saunter behind New Buildings down Addison's Walk, and afterwards spent the whole night talking in Lewis's rooms.

Soon afterwards, on October 18, 1931, he wrote to his old friend Greeves saying, "What Dyson and Tolkien showed me was this: that if I met the idea of sacrifice in a Pagan story I didn't mind it at all: again, that if I met the idea of a god sacrificing himself to himself . . . I liked it very much and was mysteriously moved by it: again, that the idea of the dying and reviving god (Balder, Adonis, Bacchus) similarly moved me provided I met it anywhere *except* in the Gospels. The reason was that in Pagan stories I was prepared to feel the myth as profound and suggestive of meanings beyond my grasp even tho' I could not say in cold prose 'what it meant.' Now the story of Christ is simply a true myth: a myth working on us in the same say as the others, but with this tremendous difference that *it really happened.*"[30]

But even before Lewis could get off his letter to Greeves he had drawn his final conclusions to the whole episode. He and Warnie had taken on September 28 a picnic lunch to Whipsnade Zoo in Warnie's motor-cycle and sidecar:

"When we set out I did not believe that Jesus Christ is the Son of God, and when we reached the zoo I did . . . It was . . . like when a man, after long sleep, still lying motionless in bed, becomes aware that he is now awake . . .

"And what, in conclusion, of Joy? . . . It was valuable only as a pointer to something other and outer. While that other was in doubt, the pointer naturally loomed large in my thoughts. When we are lost in the woods the sight of a signpost is a great matter. He who first sees it cries, 'Look!' The whole party gathers round and stares. But when we have found the road and are passing signposts every few miles, we shall not stop and stare. They will encourage us and we shall be grateful to the authority that set them up. But we shall not stop and stare, or not much; not on this road, though their pillars are of silver and their lettering of gold. 'We would be at Jerusalem.'

"Not, of course, that I don't often catch myself stopping to stare at roadside objects of even less importance."[31]

PART III
Beyond Ivory Towers

Magdalen College deer park and New Buildings, in which
Lewis had his rooms

LEWIS WAS NOW ENTERING THE BUSIEST PERIOD of his life. As a Christian, the shackles of ambition fell away. It didn't matter to him any more that he was a failed poet: he now had something very important to say and he was eager to get on with writing about the things he most enjoyed. Indeed, now that he no longer cared about "making a name for himself" he wrote with an ease he had never known before. His first prose work, *The Pilgrim's Regress* (1933), an allegorical account of the part Joy played in his conversion, was written during a fortnight's holiday with Arthur Greeves. Then, by the end of 1935 he had completed the work which established him at once as one of the greatest literary scholars of his generation—*The Allegory of Love: A Study in Medieval Tradition* (1936).

Writing about it in *The Times Literary Supplement*, the reviewer of *The Allegory of Love*, adding one bouquet to another, said of the chapter on Chaucer's *Troilus and Criseyde*: "Mr. Lewis reaches his full stature as a critic. His appreciation of Chaucer's marvellous poem is of the very highest quality—the proof, if the reader of his book needs any, that the historical method, in the hands of one who can keep imaginative control of the facts, adds depth to appreciation while taking nothing from its immediacy."[1]

Shortly afterwards there poured from his pen his science fiction trilogy, *Out of the Silent Planet* (1938), *Perelandra* (1943), and *That Hideous Strength* (1945) from which Lewis discovered that any amount of theology can be smuggled into people's minds under cover of romance without their knowing it. Without intending any deception, so perfectly imagined were the first two stories, set on Mars and Venus, that, in answering his fan mail, Lewis had constantly to deny that he had ever travelled in space.

Throughout this time friends gathered round Lewis. It started with Tolkien on Monday mornings as far back as 1931 and gathered momentum through the years until by 1939 there were regular Thursday evening meetings in Magdalen during term time and again on Tuesdays in the "Eagle and Child" pub—or the "Bird and Baby" as it's called. There they drank beer and discussed, among other things, whatever writings they had read aloud at the Thursday evening gatherings.

Warnie—or Major Lewis, as he was after twenty years in the army —had retired to live with his brother at The Kilns in 1932. When he was called back into active service at the outbreak of World War II, Jack kept him informed about the activities of the club. Writing to him on November 11, 1939, he said:

"On Thursday we had a meeting of the Inklings . . . We dined at the Eastgate. I have never in my life seen Dyson so exuberant—'A roaring

Mrs. J. K. Moore's first meeting with the Lewis family, at the home of Mr. and Mrs. Joseph Lewis, Fisherwick House, Newcastle, Northern Ireland, August 1934. *First row, left to right:* Beth Lewis, Ranald Muir, Joan Lewis, Alex Muir. *Back row:* Maureen Moore, Ida Lewis, Rev. Ranald Muir, Mrs. M.T. Lewis, Mrs. J. K. Moore, Martha Muir, Sarah Jane Lewis, W. H. Lewis, C. S. Lewis

The main quad of the Bodleian Library

cataract of nonsense.' The bill of fare afterwards, consisted of a section of the new Hobbit book from Tolkien, a nativity play from Charles Williams (unusually intelligible for him, and approved by all), and a chapter out of a book on The Problem of Pain from me . . . The subject matter of the three readings formed almost a logical sequence, and produced a really first-rate evening's talk of the usual wide-ranging kind—'from grave to gay, from lively to severe.' "[2]

An employee of the Oxford University Press, Charles Williams moved from London to Oxford with other members of the press at the outbreak of the war. Lewis arranged for him to give a series of lectures on Milton, and on February 11, 1940, Jack wrote to Warnie about the second of Williams's lectures in the Divinity School of the Bodleian: "On Monday Charles Williams lectured, nominally on Comus but really on Chastity. Simply as criticism it was superb—because here was a man who really cared with every fiber of his being about 'The sage and serious doctrine of virginity' which it would never occur to the ordinary modern critic to take seriously. But it was more important still as a

Some of the Inklings at "The Trout," outside Oxford, c. 1940.
Left to right: Commander James Dundas-Grant, Colin Hardie,
Dr. R. E. Havard, CSL, and Peter Havard (Dr. Havard's son)

sermon. It was a beautiful sight to see a whole roomful of modern young men and women sitting in that absolute silence which can *not* be faked."[3] Shortly afterwards, March 3, 1940, he wrote to Warnie with the news that "A visit from Dyson on Thursday produced a meeting of all the Inklings except yourself and Barfield . . . Dyson . . . was in his usual form and on being told of Williams' Milton lectures on 'the sage and serious doctrine of virginity,' replied 'The fellow's becoming a common *chastitute.*' "[4]

Walter Hooper and Dr. Robert Havard, or "Humphrey" as Lewis renamed him, met for a pint of beer in the Bird and Baby pub at lunchtime on July 17, 1978, to reminisce about Humphrey's earliest meetings with Jack Lewis and the Inklings. He remembered their first meeting, in fact, very well:

I inherited a practice in Oxford and among the patients handed over to me was Jack. He got the 'flu and I went to him and we spent 25 minutes discussing Thomas Aquinas who I was interested in at the time and Jack picked up the interest and the 25 minutes passed in a flash. This was my first impression of him and his way of handling his medical complaints. It was not long after that that he described to me this group of friends that met at Magdalen on Thursday evenings and it was then, I think, that he asked if I would care to join them.

The Inklings meetings were far from consistent affairs. They varied very much according to who was there. They were a varied group. They didn't all come, and always things depended on what sort of dinner they had had. Some of us had dined well, some less well. Warnie would make tea—I think it was one of the first things—and this was handed round and after we had had a cup or two of tea we read our stuff if we had got any stuff to read. After this we went on to bottled beer . . . We used to discuss literary things quite seriously. I mean, somebody would read something and there would be a quite serious discussion about it.

Caricature of Warren by Clive,
c. July 14, 1930

Jack and Warnie at Annagassan, Ireland, 1949

The point which one chiefly remembers about these meetings is their humour, their hilarity. For instance there were *The Screwtape Letters*. Jack read them, they were literary productions, and we cheered and we laughed. We said how much we had enjoyed them. To that extent we criticised them seriously and if there had been anything to find fault with, we'd have found fault. But the chief effect of *The Screwtape Letters* was laughter, and how very successful a medium he had managed to find for saying what he wanted to say —original and successful. They really set us going. We were more or less rolling off our chairs.

Jack shared quite a bit with Doctor Johnson. He could be overbearing, he could be quite rude on occasion; he was always witty, he had a memory, a fantastic memory. He could quote poetry by the yard straight off the reel without hesitation and he could make up poetry as he went along so you were never quite sure whether he was quoting or whether he was making it up, and this he would do deliberately on occasions to fox us.

I remember a meeting that particularly stands out; not that Jack took himself any very great part, but he was the cause of the evenings. There was a doctor [Warfield M. Firor] in America who was very impressed by his writings and just after the war, when food was very short, he used to send Jack hams. Jack being Jack, he invited us round to what he called a "ham evening" and these were very popular as you can imagine. And then, one great evening, the doctor himself was over and attended. The fellow astounded us by a story he told of an adventure in Russia in which he pretended to be the husband of a Russian lady who wanted to escape to the West, which the law, apparently, would then allow. But the doctor already had a wife in the United States, which was a bit embarrassing. But it didn't prevent him going in and getting the lady out. We all felt that this was one of the coldest acts of courage we had all heard of for a long time.

There is another story which stands out too. David Mathew, Gervase's brother, was a brilliant raconteur and came one evening. He was, at that time, a roving Archbishop over the whole of Africa and had many good stories to tell of his experiences there. In one of his visits he made friends with a tribe and especially the Chief. Unfortunately the Chief died and left all his possessions to his friend David Mathew. The awkward thing was that he found amongst these some fifty *wives* which, for a Roman Catholic Archbishop, is a bit of a problem. He told us how he worked his way out of that one though, and amused us a great deal in the process.

Following the publication of Lewis's *The Problem of Pain* in 1940, the Director of Religious Broadcasting of the BBC asked him to give a series of talks over the air in 1942. Lewis accepted because he regarded England as part of that vast "post-Christian" world which thought it had rejected Christianity when, in truth, it had never been told what it

CSL looking west from his sitting-room in New Buildings onto the
Magdalen College deer park, 1947

CSL standing in his study in New Buildings, Magdalen College, 1947

is about. These talks, given between the years 1942 and 1944, were typical of Lewis's extraordinary lucidity of expression and inexorable logic, and were afterwards published as *Mere Christianity* (1952). In an indirect attack against the slush talked by liberal theologians, he said in one of the talks:

"I am trying here to prevent anyone saying the really foolish thing that people often say about Him: 'I'm ready to accept Jesus as a great moral teacher, but I don't accept His claim to be God.' That is the one thing we must not say. A man who was merely a man and said the sort of things Jesus said would not be a great moral teacher. He would either be a lunatic—on a level with the man who says he is a poached egg— or else he would be the Devil of Hell. You must make your choice. Either this man was, and is, the Son of God: or else a madman or something worse. You can shut Him up for a fool, you can spit at Him and kill Him as a demon; or you can fall at His feet and call Him Lord and God. But let us not come with any patronising nonsense about His

Walter Hooper and Dr. Havard in "The Bird and Baby"

The undersigned, having just partaken of your ham, have drunk your health:

C. S. Lewis. Fellow of Magdalen, sometime scholar of University College late 13ᵉ Light Infantry

H. V. D. Dyson   Fellow of Merton College, Lecturer of University College, University Lecturer in English Literature. ~~Formerly~~ sometime Lecturer of Exeter College. Queen's Own Royal West Kent Regt 1915-19.

David Cecil   Fellow of New College — ex-Fellow of Wadham College — University Lecturer in English Literature. Commoner of Christ Church.

W. H. Lewis.   Royal Military College, Sandhurst, Regular Army 1914-1932, World War II 1939-45. Major, Retired pay.

Colin Hardie   Fellow and Tutor in Classics of Magdalen College University Lecturer in Greek and Latin Literature, formerly Director of the British School at Rome, and Fellow, Scholar & Exhibitioner of Balliol College Secretary of the Oxford Dante Society (founded 1878) Sector Warden A.R.P. service Oxford.

Christopher · Reuel · Tolkien :·   B. A. :· Undergraduate, of Trinity College :· [late R.A.F. & R.N.V.R]

R Emlyn Harvard   M. A. · D.M. Oxon. B.A. Cantab. late Scholar & Research Fellow University of Oxford, late Lecturer in Physiology Guy's Hospital; Demias tutor in Biochemistry University of Oxford, late Surgeon R.N.V.R.

John Ronald Reuel Tolkien   M. A. Merton Professor of English Language & Literature, late professor of Anglo-Saxon (Pembroke College), and exhibitioner of Exeter College, and of the Lancashire Fusiliers (1914-8) and father of the above-named C.R.T.

The Inklings' letter of appreciation to Dr. Warfield M. Firor

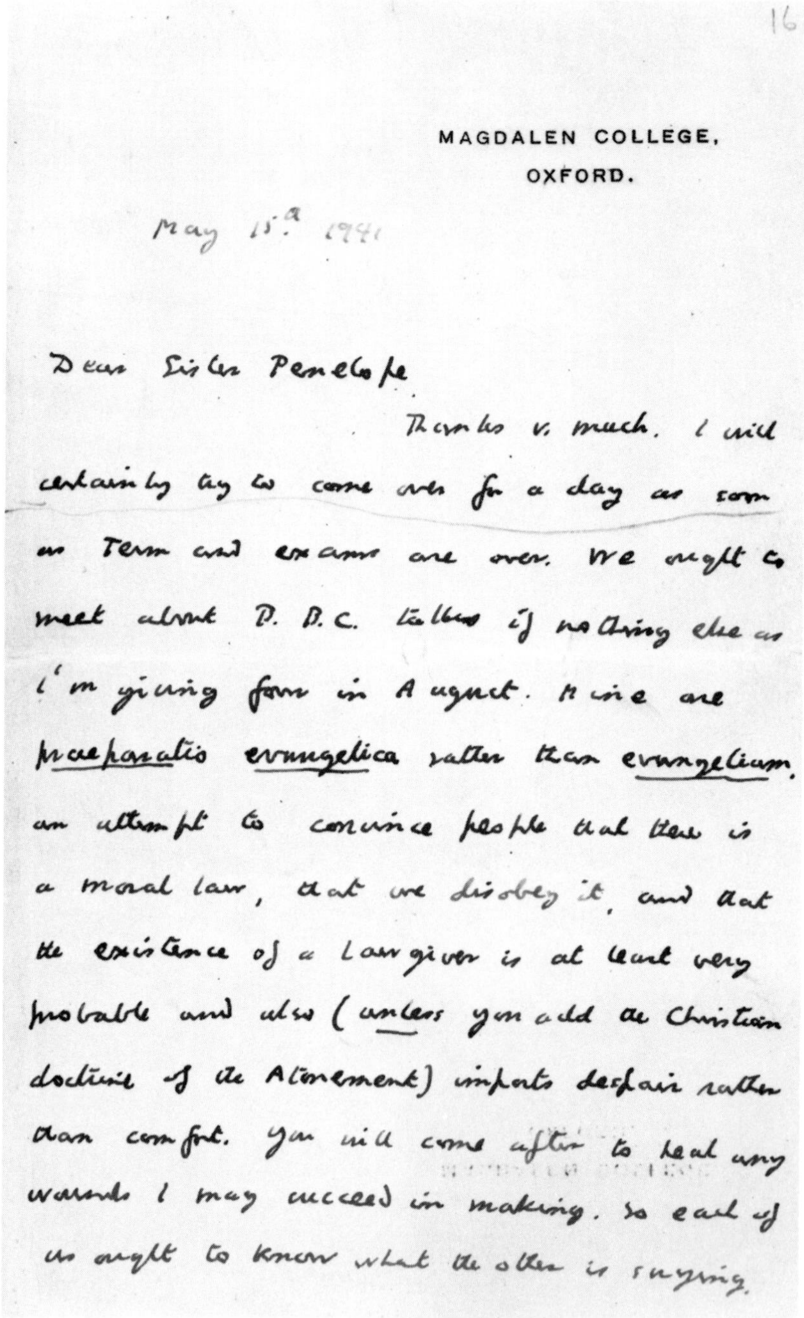

MAGDALEN COLLEGE,
OXFORD.

May 15ª 1941

Dear Sister Penelope

Thanks v. much. I will certainly try to come over for a day as soon as Term and exams are over. We ought to meet about B. B. C. talks if nothing else as I'm giving four in August. Mine are _praeparatio_ _evangelica_ rather than _evangelium_, an attempt to convince people that there is a moral law, that we disobey it, and that the existence of a Lawgiver is at least very probable and also (_unless_ you add the Christian doctrine of the Atonement) imports despair rather than comfort. You will come after to heal any wounds I may succeed in making. So each of us ought to know what the other is saying.

Letter to Sister Penelope Lawson

I've given some talks to the R.A.F. at Abingdon already and as far as I can judge they were a complete failure. I await instructions from the Chaplain in Chief about the Vacation. Ye---jobs one dare neither refuse nor perform. One must take comfort in remembering that god used an _ass_ to convert the prophet: perhaps if we do our poor best we shall be allowed a stall near it in the celestial stable — rather like this!

yours sincerely

C. S. Lewis

being a great human teacher. He has not left that open to us. He did not intend to."[5]

In between broadcasts Lewis was travelling all over the country lecturing on theology to the Royal Air Force, and at Oxford he accepted the demands of those who were clamouring for an open forum for the discussion of the intellectual difficulties connected with Christianity. Lewis was elected President of the Socratic Club on its formation in 1941, and from then on Socratic posters were pinned up in every college. Meetings were held every Monday evening in term; the first one being in Somerville College on the evening of January 26, 1942, when Humphrey Havard read a paper answering the question "Won't Mankind Outgrow Christianity in the Face of the Advance of Science and of Modern Ideologies?" Somerville happened to be the college of Lewis's friend, Dorothy L. Sayers, who was herself a member of the Socratic.

During the meetings Christians and atheists were both given a chance to argue the pros and cons of the Christian religion. Lewis was the gladiator and could always be depended upon to uphold orthodox, supernatural Christianity. Hence the students flocked to watch him wipe the floor with any liberal or atheist intrepid enough to step into the arena with him. Much as Lewis relished "rational opposition," he

Socratic Club poster

Oxford University

SOCRATIC CLUB

President: C. S. LEWIS, M.A.

This Club has been formed for those who do not necessarily wish to commit themselves to Christian views but are interested in a philosophical approach to religion in general and to Christianity in particular, in a spirit of free enquiry and in the light of modern thought and knowledge.

OPEN DISCUSSION will follow the introduction of the subjects by speakers who will include both Christians and non-Christians.

MEETINGS

Michaelmas Term, 1945

Oct. 15th. (S. HILDA'S)	The Nature of Reason	Mr. C. S. LEWIS
Oct. 22nd. (S. HILDA'S)	The Nature of Faith	Rev. A. WHITEHOUSE
Oct. 29th. (S. HILDA'S)	The Existence of God	Rev. E. L. MASCALL / Rev. JOHN MARSH
Nov. 5th. (ORIEL)	Was Christ Divine?	Prof. L. HODGSON / A Unitarian
Nov. 12th. (ORIEL)	Has Man a Soul?	Prof. H. H. PRICE / Dr. A. M. FARRER
Nov. 19th. (S. JOHN'S)	The Empirical Basis of Moral Obligation	Dr. R. EISLER / Mr. CARRITT (we hope)
Nov. 26th. (MAGDALEN)	Marxist and Christian views of the Nature of Man / Joint Meeting with the O.U. Socialist Club.	Mr. A. ROBERTSON / Prof. E. CAMMAERTS
Dec. 3rd. (S. JOHN'S)	The Atomic Bomb—and After	Dr. DAVID EVANS

Meetings at 8.15 p.m. on MONDAYS.

The Papers will be followed by Questions and Open Discussion.

Pulpit from which Lewis delivered the sermon "The Weight of Glory"

was never without humour and many Socratic members still recall the evening on which the first speaker was a relativist who is said to have ended his talk with the assertion: "The world does not exist, Oxford does not exist, and I am confident that *I* do not exist!" When Lewis was asked to reply, he stood up and said, "How am I to talk to a man who's *not there?*"[6]

Perhaps the greatest accolade given Lewis was the invitation to preach the University Sermon in the thirteenth-century Church of St. Mary the Virgin. The pulpit from which he delivered that sermon— "The Weight of Glory"—is the same as that of Latimer, Newman, and Keble. In front of a packed church with people even in the windows Lewis's words on June 8, 1941, were beyond anyone's expectations:

". . . It is a serious thing to live in a society of possible gods and goddesses, to remember that the dullest and most uninteresting person you talk to may one day be a creature which, if you saw it now, you would be strongly tempted to worship, or else a horror and a corruption such as you now meet, if at all, only in a nightmare. All day long we are, in some degree, helping each other to one or other of these destinations. It is in the light of these overwhelming possibilities, it is with the awe and the circumspection proper to them, that we should conduct all our dealings with one another, all friendships, all loves, all play, all

CSL in his sitting-room in Magdalen College, December 21, 1949. With only a coal fire and an electric heater—there being no central heating—Lewis usually wore a dressing gown over his clothes when giving tutorials and entertaining during the winter.

politics. There are no *ordinary* people. You have never talked to a mere mortal. Nations, cultures, arts, civilisations—these are mortal, and their life is to ours as the life of a gnat. But it is immortals whom we joke with, work with, marry, snub, and exploit—immortal horrors or everlasting splendours. This does not mean that we are to be perpetually solemn. We must play. But our merriment must be of that kind (and it is, in fact, the merriest kind) which exists between people who have, from the outset, taken each other seriously—no flippancy, no superiority, no presumption. And our charity must be a real and costly love, with deep feeling for the sins in spite of which we love the sinner—no mere tolerance or indulgence which parodies love as flippancy parodies merriment. Next to the Blessed Sacrament itself, your neighbour is the holiest object presented to your senses. If he is your Christian neighbour he is holy in almost the same way, for in him also Christ *vere latitat*— the glorifier and the glorified, Glory Himself, is truly hidden."[7]

And Lewis lived what he preached. Walter Hooper remembered a

J. R. R. Tolkien, Miramar Hotel, Bournemouth, April 13, 1971

Father John Tolkien and Miss Priscilla Tolkien

conversation they had about a bore whom they both knew: "We were talking one day about a man who was generally recognised as being almost unbelievably dull. I told Lewis that the man succeeded in interesting me by the very intensity of his boredom. 'Yes,' he said, 'but let us not forget that Our Lord might well have said "As ye have done it unto one of the least of these my bores, ye have done it unto me." ' There was a twinkle in his eye as he said it and we both laughed, yet knowing at the same time that it was no joke. On another occasion I mentioned that I knew of a man's grave, the epitaph on whose gravestone read 'Here lies an atheist, all dressed up but with nowhere to go.' To which Lewis replied, 'I bet he wishes that were so!' "

Another literary giant of this age was his good friend Professor J. R. R. Tolkien, whose "new Hobbit book" which he read in instalments to the Inklings, was later published, with much encouragement from Lewis, as *The Lord of the Rings*. Tolkien was the Merton Professor of English Literature, whose chair was attached to Merton College.

On June 29, 1978, Tolkien's son, Father John Tolkien, and Father Tolkien's sister, Priscilla, met with Walter Hooper in the garden of Priscilla's Oxford home. So it was, then, that over tea they discussed some of the most pleasant recollections of their association with Lewis:

Martin Moynihan giving a talk
about CSL to the Brasenose
College Stamford Club

"I suppose," remembered Priscilla, "he was almost at the height of
his fame, or beginning to be—the height of his fame as a great scholar
that is, as distinct perhaps from his theological fame—when I was an
undergraduate at Oxford. His lectures were certainly enormously popular and I think that I attended the whole course of his Prolegomena to
Medieval and Renaissance Literature where, as far as I remember, there
used to be a vast audience and one had to be very early to get a good
place. It was like a great performance. Apart from the intrinsic interest
and the splendid manner of delivery, I had a very personal reason for

CSL, 1938

Lewis's Parish Church

remembering one incident particularly well. He was the sort of lecturer that did think of the needs of small people like ourselves, people who knew very little and who wanted to take down in manageable form the very considerable learning which he was putting over to us. I can remember on this particular occasion he was telling us in marvellously lucid and simplified form the great names throughout the ages who had been important in developing theories of Art and Literature, and these great names like Aristotle and Milton and Dryden were rolling down through the Examination Schools because his voice, I seem to remember, was very splendid and carried very easily. There was a pause and finally he said, 'And lastly we have the Tolkienian theory of sub-creation.' Now that really did puzzle me because, whereas I had read a little Aristotle and a little Dryden, I couldn't think what 'Tolkienian' referred

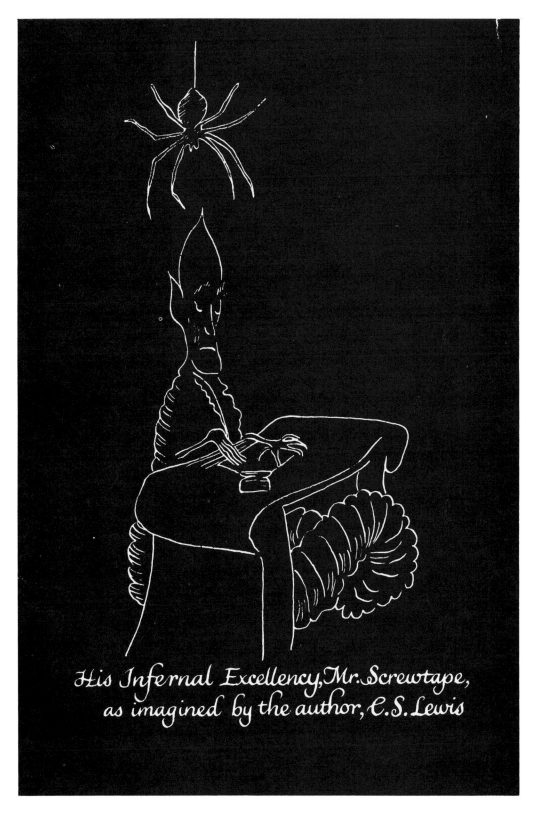

His Abysmal Sublimity Under-Secretary Screwtape, as
imagined by the author, C. S. Lewis

Three photographs of a relaxed Lewis in his Magdalen College rooms to and was chewing my pen before writing a suitable note when a friend of mine of the same age as myself—that is, we had reached the very advanced age of about nineteen—jogged me in the side and said, with intense excitement: '*He's* talking about *your* father!'

"I also remember the marvellous marmalade story recorded by my father who, apparently to his great surprise and concern, saw Lewis walking in the centre of Oxford one day with a large black armband. And feeling that this must mean that he was lately and very heavily bereaved, said, with what he hoped was suitable concern, 'I am very sorry. Is it someone close to you?' To which Lewis replied: 'No, it is Mrs. Moore's marmalade-making season and I am plagued with wasps!' "

Father John Tolkien remembered Lewis mostly for his joviality and his talk: "We talked about all sorts of things including botany. He was always interested in anything that arose and wanted always to follow it up. Apparently he didn't know that some plants had their male and their female characteristics on different plants, of which the yew is one. And at about that time of the year I was home—sometime in March or

Mill Pond of Magdalen College, Oxford

CSL's rooms in Magdalen College
as they are now

thereabouts when they flower—and my father and I were on a walk when we met Jack coming in the opposite direction. There at the entrance to the drive down to Holywell Manor was Jack in his deerstalker hat beating two yew bushes with his walking stick to find out which was male and which female, and then when the male gave out clouds of pollen, he said, 'Got you!' Then he saw us.

"But I remember the last time we saw him. My father had expressed a wish to see him and I had a car at the time. It was about three months before he died and we drove over to The Kilns for what turned out to be a very excellent time together for about an hour. I remember the conversation was very much about the *Morte d'Arthur* and whether trees died."

And it is interesting to recall that Martin Moynihan in his talk to the Brasenose Stamford Club was also greatly taken by Lewis's talk. "What a pleasure," Mr. Moynihan said, "those evenings were when,

Lewis's own drawing of Narnia

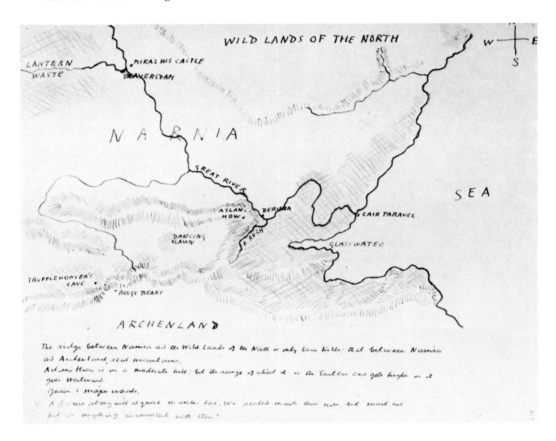

Pauline Baynes

round his fire, with a mug of ale, we would all read aloud some Old English epic—but there's only one—*Beowulf*. And then, after that, what talk, what cut and thrust, on any subject that came up.

"Once, someone asked him what he thought of Divine Right. Lewis said he wasn't sure the Stuarts had been very good monarchs. However, he said he supposed doctrine had a high derivation—indeed from St. Peter's words that the powers that be are ordained of God. 'Oh, I don't believe in God,' said one of the others. Some laughed. Anyway, the objector said, 'What do you mean by "God"?' I thought Lewis might have been halted, or have shied off. But no. 'Well, God,' he said, 'is a self-subsistent Being: creator of all things: dependent on none.' It was as if you'd been listening to a Schoolman—Aquinas, as it were, or Duns Scotus.

"But, of course, deeper than any debate or mere philosophy was

Plots.

SHIP. Two children somehow get on board a ship of ancient build. Discover presently that they are sailing in time (backward): the captain will bring them to islands that have not existed for millennia. Approach islands. Attacked by enemies. Children captured. Discover that the first captain was really taking them because his sick king needs blood of a boy in the far future. Nevertheless prefer the captain and his side to their wd-discard rescuers. Escape + return to their first hosts. The blood giving, not fatal, + happy ending. Various islands (of Odyssey + St Brendan) can be thrown in. Beauty of the ship the central appeal. To be a v. green + pearly thing

PICTURE. A magic picture. One of the children gets thro' the frame into the picture + one of the creatures gets out of the picture into our world.

INVENTED Ordinary fairy-tale e.g. Q. who erupts a child for our end.

SEQUEL TO L.W.W. The present tyrants to be then. Intervening history of Narnia told nominally by the Dwarf but really an abstract of his views wh. amounts to telling it in my own person.

Plot outline for *The Voyage of the Dawn Treader*

some inner thing. As was so of Johnson also. It made him a bit awesome. It was a sense of honour at first. Which, later, became an act of faith. Lewis was fond of quoting Patmore, on conversion. It is like a man marching along. Suddenly a band strikes up. The man is still marching. But now he is marching in tune . . .

"Home from Delhi in the late 40s—Old Delhi, where I had come across the privately printed poems of John Meade Falkner. I went to seek out Meade Falkner's grave. I found it at Burford, an altar-tomb in the graveyard. It was darkling and I could scarcely make out the lettering around the tomb. Latin. No quotation marks. No indication of source. Latin I could not place:

Ego dormio sed cor meum vigilat

"I went on to Oxford, called on Lewis, received a warm welcome and, before I left, told him of my find. What did he make of the inscription? We were back at 'contexts.' Immediately he took it on. And you could see him getting it, until we allowed the meaning, in its totality, to be our farewell. '*Ego dormio*—I am sleeping—*sed cor meum*—but my heart—*vigilat*—is watching . . . wakes . . . waketh! It is the Shulamite! It is from the Song of Songs:

I sleep but my heart waketh.'

"I said good-night, went across the lawn, through the Cloisters and out into The High."

It was at his parish church—The Church of the Holy Trinity—not far from The Kilns in Headington Quarry that at the 8:00 A.M. Mass on Sunday, July 20, 1940, the book which brought him international fame was conceived.

Writing to Warnie on that day he said: "Before the service was over —one could wish these things came more seasonably—I was struck by an idea for a book which I think might be both useful and entertaining. It would be called *As One Devil to Another* and would consist of letters from an elderly retired devil to a young devil who has just started work on his first 'patient.' The idea would be to give all the psychology of temptation from the *other* point of view."[8]

The title was in fact *The Screwtape Letters* (1942) as Lewis decided to make the elderly devil a prominent official in the Infernal Civil Service—"His Abysmal Sublimity Under-Secretary Screwtape" and the young devil became Wormwood, who is Screwtape's nephew. Worm-

CSL in his Magdalen College sitting-room, December 21, 1949

Lewis was featured on the cover of Time September 8, 1947,
in recognition of his popularity with Americans

A detailed study of CSL's face made in his study in Magdalen College wood is engaged in his first assignment on Earth, which is to secure the damnation of a young man who has just become a Christian. The reader must, however, throughout the book, keep looking at things in reverse. Instead of asking what we think of devils, imagine what *they* think and say about us. "Our Father Below" is Satan, and "The Enemy" is of course—by the same reversal—God. All the thirty-one letters are "useful and entertaining," but here is one of Screwtape's most insidious bits of advice to Wormwood:

> Like all young tempters, you are anxious to report spectacular wickedness. But do remember, the only thing that matters is the extent to which you separate the man from the Enemy. It does not matter how small the sins are provided that their cumulative effect is to edge the man away from the Light and out into the Nothing. Murder is no better than cards if cards can do the trick. Indeed the safest road to Hell is the gradual one—the gentle slope, soft underfoot, without sudden turnings, without milestones, without signposts.
>
> Your affectionate uncle,
Screwtape[9]

The *Screwtape Letters* now soars with the classics. And yet knowing this, with typical humility Lewis wrote: "Some have paid me an undeserved compliment by supposing that my *Letters* were the ripe fruit of many years' study in moral and ascetic theology. They forgot that there is an equally reliable, though less creditable, way of learning how temptation works. 'My heart'—I need no other's—'sheweth me the wickedness of the ungodly.' "[10]

If there are those who imagine that Lewis laid too great emphasis on the pains of Hell as opposed to the joys of Heaven, they have only to read *The Problem of Pain* and, amongst the many other works he wrote in the 1940s, *The Great Divorce* (1945) to see that it is quite the other way round. But of course the perceptive reader will have noticed that this is so even of *The Screwtape Letters*, of which even that one-time formidable atheist, Professor C. E. M. Joad, felt compelled to admit that "Mr. Lewis possesses the rare gift of making righteousness readable."[11]

It was by the mill pond at the back of Magdalen that he had walked with Tolkien and Dyson on that wild, windy night of his conversion, and daily now he took this route home—where increasingly his problems mounted. Though Mrs. Moore had a number of detractors, not once in all the thirty-two years that he had looked after her did Lewis ever say a word against her. As for Warnie, he had since the mid-1940s been sliding into serious alcoholism, the whole burden of his welfare

CSL at Magdalen College, November 25, 1950

falling upon his brother Jack. Yet with all this Lewis continued to write well.

Not only fine pieces of literature but day-to-day letters to those who wrote to him, even to the day of his death. Every letter was answered by return of post, often with more care than was lavished on the enquiry.

For him, writing was his recreation, his solace, as natural as breathing: and without turning his back on any of his troubles he produced some of the most pleasant books of his whole career—the *Chronicles of Narnia.* They were the unexpected creation of his middle age and seem to be his greatest claim to immortality, setting him high in that particular branch of literature in which few attain more than a transitory or an esoteric fame—somewhere on the same shelf as Lewis Carroll and E. Nesbit and George MacDonald, as Kipling, Kenneth Grahame and Andrew Lang: a branch of literature in which there are relatively few great classics but in which, as he himself said, "the good ones last." The final of the seven books—*The Last Battle*—won the Carnegie Medal, but Lewis, typically, gave much of the credit to the illustrator, then still a young woman in her early twenties—Pauline Baynes.

Pauline Baynes now lives in Surrey and on a visit to her cottage

Aslan the Lion, as depicted by
Pauline Baynes

there on July 19, 1978, Walter Hooper asked her to describe her earliest contact with Lewis.

"I wondered why," she said, "I had this marvellous chance of drawing for someone who was so well known, a household word, C. S. Lewis. And he told me that he had actually gone into a bookshop and asked the assistant there if she could recommend someone who could draw children and animals. I don't know whether he was just being kind to me and making me feel that I was more important than I was, or whether he had simply heard about me from his friend Tolkien."

As to the Christian parallels between the stories and the Gospels, she said, "I didn't see it at all until after I had finished drawing *The Lion, the Witch and the Wardrobe,* but I must admit that when I was drawing Aslan going through all the awfulnesses, when he was being tortured, I was crying all the time."

PART IV

Christians Never Say Good-bye

The Kilns, built in 1922, as it looked in 1963. The property in which the house is set was in 1881 used for the quarrying of clay for the making of bricks. The pit from which the clay was dug had by 1930 become a pond. The house itself took its name from the brick kilns which stood nearby. They were demolished in 1964 because they were considered unsafe.

At the same time that Miss Baynes was struck by the sufferings of Aslan, Lewis had his own "awfulnesses" to cope with. Mrs. Moore, his "adopted mother" of so many years, was now an invalid in need of much care. This would not have been so difficult for Lewis had he been able to count on his brother's help. But Warnie was himself in need of help. Over the years his alcoholism had become very serious, his bouts of drinking more frequent. As long as he was in Oxford, Lewis could get him into a nursing home when the drinking bouts became unmanageable. But now, more and more often, Warnie was slipping out of his brother's control by going to Ireland where the licensing hours of the pubs were virtually non-existent. And so it went on. With Mrs. Moore requiring constant attention, and with no one to help him, Lewis—weary to the bone—found it impossible to squeeze in a much-needed holiday. In April 1950 Mrs. Moore had to be admitted to a nursing home. Even so, she continued to rely on Lewis who visited her every day till, at the age of seventy-nine, she died on January 12, 1951.

While Lewis begged those who knew her to pray for her soul, there was nevertheless some relief in being thus freed from the strain of the last few years. Lewis and Arthur Greeves began planning a spring holiday in Ireland, and in his letter to Arthur on March 23, 1951, Lewis said: "Looking forward!—yes, I can't keep the feeling within bounds. I know how a bottle of champagne feels while the wire is being taken off the cork. Pop!"[1]

Indeed, Lewis was to enjoy a freedom he had not known since his undergraduate days. And he was full of creative energy. It was while he was writing the Narnian stories that he found time to complete the most

ambitious of his scholarly works—his thorough and immensely readable *English Literature in the Sixteenth Century* (1954).

It is perhaps not without irony that not long after Mrs. Moore's
death Lewis was to meet another woman who was to play a significant
part in his life. This was the writer Joy Davidman, wife of the American
novelist William Gresham. Both Greshams had been converted to Christianity by Lewis's books. But Joy was interested in more than Lewis's
writings and, leaving her husband and two sons in New York, she
turned up at The Kilns in September 1952. It was soon apparent that
Joy had other ideas than those of simple intellectual friendship and
Lewis took fright. Meanwhile, Joy learned that William Gresham had
formed an intimate attachment to the woman left in charge of her children. She returned to New York in January 1953, and after allowing her

Alan Sorrell's painting *Conversation Piece,* 1954, in which CSL is shown
with some of the other dons in the Senior Common Room of Magdalen
College, Oxford. *Clockwise, from left front:* Alan Raitt, Colin Hardie, A. W.
Adams, Gilbert Ryle, T. S. R. Boase, Godfrey Driver, C. S. Lewis, James
Griffiths, and J. A. W. Bennett.

Joy Davidman at The Kilns

husband to divorce her on grounds of desertion, she returned the following summer with her sons to England. Joy settled in Belsize Park, London, and sent her sons David (b. 1944) and Douglas (b. 1945) to Dane Court, a preparatory school in Surrey. It was during this time that Joy Davidman wrote *Smoke on the Mountain* (1955)—an interpretation of the Ten Commandments. Eventually in 1955, after a number of weekend visits to Oxford to see Lewis, and because of a very strong desire to be close to him, she moved to Oxford and set up house at 10 Old High Street, Headington.

It had long been clear that Oxford was showing a marked ingratitude in not electing Lewis to a professorship in the University he had served so long. But at that time a man's fame outside the University often served as a considerable drawback *within* it. Professor J. R. R. Tolkien explained it to Walter Hooper thus: "No Oxford don was forgiven for writing books outside his field of study—except for detective stories which dons, like everyone else, read when they are down with the 'flu. But it was considered unforgiveable that Lewis wrote international best-sellers, and worse still that many were of a religious nature." Oxford's behaviour is, nevertheless, difficult to defend as Lewis did not neglect his "field of study" and was then, as now, considered one of the world's foremost literary critics. But all this was soon to change in a manner that surprised everyone.

In 1954 Cambridge University advertised a new Professorship of Medieval and Renaissance English Literature, a chair which—interestingly—was to be attached to Magdalene College, Cambridge. The chair was founded with Lewis in view as its first occupant, and Cambridge's

Cambridge

Photograph commissioned by the National Portrait Gallery to
commemorate Lewis's appointment to the Chair of Medieval and
Renaissance English Literature in Cambridge University, 1955

Professor of English, Basil Willey, anxious that Lewis should apply, wrote to him saying "Come over into Macedonia and help us!"[2] Tolkien, who was on the Cambridge board of electors, thought Lewis the obvious choice, and though he and other Oxford friends urged Lewis to apply, it was for Lewis a difficult decision. Eventually, after much encouragement, he applied—and was accepted. Those familiar with the two great English universities will best understand why Lewis decided as he did. A tutor's life can be very tiring as he not only has to tutor nearly all day but (in many instances) give public lectures as well. The holder of a professorial chair only gives public lectures, thus leav-

King's College, Cambridge, and the River Cam

The spires of Cambridge

ing him with much more time for research. Contrary to much that is said, Lewis *liked* tutoring. Even so, after nearly thirty years of listening to undergraduate essays, he was ready for the change. Writing to Sister Penelope on June 30, 1954, he said, "Yes, I've been made Professor of Medieval and Renaissance English at Cambridge. The scope of the Chair (a new one) suits me exactly. But it won't be as big a change as you might think. I shall still live in Oxford in the Vac., and on weekends in the term. My address will be Magdalene, so I remain under the same patroness. This is nice because it saves 'Admin.' readjustments in Heaven; also I can't help feeling that the dear lady [St. Mary Magdalen] understands my constitution better than a stranger would."[3]

Though Lewis was not to move from Oxford to Cambridge until January 7, 1955, he delivered his brilliantly colourful Inaugural Lecture —*De Descriptione Temporum*—on November 29, 1954. He was introduced by Dr. G. M. Trevelyan, the historian and Master of Trinity College, who told the audience that in his long experience of elections to university posts Lewis was the only one in which he had found complete unanimity of votes.

Magdalene College, Cambridge, was, like the one in Oxford, founded in the fifteenth century. But, unlike the Oxford college, Magdalene is much smaller and enjoys a long tradition of Anglo-Catholicism. Comparing them, Lewis told his friend Nevill Coghill, "I have exchanged the impenitent for the penitent Magdalen." It was in many ways a much happier change than Lewis anticipated. The status of professor not only freed him from tutorial duties, but the scope of his chair allowed him to lecture on those branches of literature closest to his heart. Cambridge received the final version of his well-known "Prolegomena to Medieval and Renaissance Literature" before those lectures were published as *The Discarded Image* (1964). A series of lectures written specially for Cambridge—*Studies in Words*—was published in 1960, to be followed the next year by *An Experiment in Criticism*.

Magdalene College, Cambridge. Lewis's rooms were those with arched windows.

Lewis in his rooms at Magdalene College, Cambridge, 1959

Almost all the letters Lewis wrote from Cambridge reflect that delight he took in the "penitent" Magdalene, and a pleasing picture of him has been supplied by Dr. Richard Ladborough, the Magdalene don who knew him best: "Lewis," he said, "was frequently jovial and delightful not only in hearing funny stories but also in telling them, and in this he was an expert. No one was less like the puritanical, tight-lipped moralist that some people thought he was after reading *The Screwtape Letters*. Some of his own stories were certainly not prudish, though never obscene. They were meant for men only and, indeed in certain respects, Lewis was what is sometimes known as 'a man's man.' He liked, for instance, to talk about his experiences in the army during World War I and to hear those of others.

His rooms in college, which with their paneling and antique appearance, could have been made attractive with little cost and even with little thought, were, it seemed to me, merely a laboratory for his work and his writings. Here he would sit with pen and ink in a hard chair before an ugly table and write for hours on end. Indeed, he seemed to be oblivious of his immediate sur-

CSL in Magdalene College, Cambridge, 1959

Jack and Joy pose for one of the first four "official" photographs made after their wedding. The Kilns, 1958. Jack, after Joy's recovery, shows signs of the pains he accepted on her behalf.

roundings, although I suppose that the beauty of them in both his universities must have had an effect upon him . . . It is now common knowledge that his memory was prodigious and that he seemed to have read everything . . .

The one author he was usually silent about was himself. Little did we know, or even guess when he dined with us in hall of an evening, that he had been engaged in penning during the daytime one of his magna opera. He was silent even when occupied in translating the Psalms into the new version. As is known, he had illustrious colleagues in this task, including, for example, T. S. Eliot. But he was unforthcoming about the whole enterprise. I think that was partly due to his modesty and to his reticence. No man was less given to name-dropping, and no one was less of a snob. If a famous person happened

Jack and Joy in front of The Kilns, with the rose arbour and
garden behind them

CSL in the circular drive of The Kilns, 1958.

CSL in the garden of The Kilns, 1958. Mrs. Michael Peto (wife of the photographer) sits with Joy under the rose arbour.

to be staying with us, and even if that person were an eminent ecclesiastic, Lewis would *appear* uninterested. Ecclesiastical gossip, indeed gossip about people at all, was completely foreign to him. More often than not he would make a point of sitting next to the most junior person in the room. He was interested in ideas and things; though, when pressed, his judgment of character was sharp and penetrating.

Until his decline in health, Lewis would go for an afternoon walk. He was good with a map and soon had tracked down most of the footpaths in and around Cambridge. Just occasionally, he would start in the morning with a visit to a pub. He liked the atmosphere of a pub, and he liked beer . . .

It seems needless to say that the chapel was the centre of his life in college. He daily attended weekday matins at 8:00 o'clock and, when he was well enough, he walked in the Fellow's Garden beforehand. He was nearly always at Oxford on weekends . . .[4]

The weekends in Oxford included Monday mornings as well. Because he had to be back in Cambridge for Tuesdays, the Inklings meetings were changed to Mondays in order to preserve the continuity and because Lewis still cared for his friends who continued to gather round him for talk, beer, and pipes in the Bird and Baby. Lewis liked Cambridge but nothing could detach his heart from Oxford which he always looked upon as home.

It will be remembered that Oxford was also the home of Joy David-

Joy at The Kilns, holding the air rifle that she used to discourage trespassers

Refreshed from their visit to Greece, Jack and Joy were
photographed by Mrs. Nickolas Zernov when she and
Professor Zernov had tea with them in the "common room"
(sitting-room) of The Kilns on May 14, 1960.

man. But for how long? She had no sooner found a house in Headington —about a mile from The Kilns—than she learned that the Home Office did not intend to renew her permit to remain in Great Britain. Though not obliged to state their reasons, it seems possible that the refusal resulted from Joy's (now much regretted) flirtation with communism in the late 1930s. Lewis spent part of September 1955 with Arthur Greeves in Ireland and talked with him about the only way he could find to help her remain in Britain—a "marriage of convenience" that would give Joy and her sons British nationality. It was explained to him that William Gresham had been married and divorced twice before he married Joy, and that even this third marriage took place before either became Christians. Still, Arthur was worried about possible consequences to Lewis if he entered into a civil contract with the lady. In replying to Arthur on October 30, 1955, Lewis said, "I don't feel the point about a 'false position.' Everyone whom it concerned wd. be told. The 'reality' wd.

CSL at Magdalene College, 1959

be, from my point of view, adultery, and therefore mustn't happen. (An easy resolution when one doesn't in the least want it!)."[5]

On April 23, 1956—shortly before Joy's permit expired—she and Lewis were "married" in the Oxford Registry Office—Joy remaining in her own home. The ceremony was largely kept secret, except from a few old friends. Lewis explained to Roger Lancelyn Green soon afterwards that the marriage was "a pure matter of friendship and expediency." Similar assurances were given his brother and others close to him.

Suddenly, as so often happens when things looked "fixed" and "over with," a small worry is replaced by a great one. Though only forty-one at the time, Joy Davidman had been suffering so terribly from pains in her left leg, diagnosed as rheumatism, that she was forced to walk with a stick. On the evening of October 18, 1956, Joy tripped and, in falling, felt the thighbone in her leg snap like a twig. She was taken to the hospital where it was discovered that the cancer which had eaten through one thighbone had spread to other parts of her body as well. It was clear to the doctors that she was dying. Though Joy seems to have taken this with heroic equanimity, it was nevertheless her desire to pass the remaining months of her life in Lewis's home. And Lewis wanted just as much to look after her. The question was *how* this could be done without damage to the lady's reputation. Writing to Greeves on November 25, 1956, Lewis disclosed the fact that Joy was dying. "In the meantime," he said, "if she gets over this bout and emerges from hospital she will no longer be fit to live alone so she must come and live here. That means (in order to avoid scandal) that our marriage must be published."[6] As a consequence, Lewis had the following announcement put in *The Times* (December 24, 1956): "A marriage has taken place between Professor C. S. Lewis, of Magdalene College, Cambridge, and Mrs. Joy Gresham, now a patient in the Churchill Hospital, Oxford. It is requested that no letters be sent." Even so, Lewis was anxious that those who knew him best not suppose that he dared go against the express teaching of Christ and the canons of the Church—that neither he nor Joy was guilty, or likely to be guilty, of adultery. That same day (December 24) he wrote to Dorothy L. Sayers, saying: "You may see in the *Times* a notice of my marriage to Joy Gresham. She is in hospital (cancer) and not likely to live; but if she gets over this go she must be given a home here. You will not think that anything wrong is going to happen. Certain problems do not arise between a dying woman and an elderly man."[7]

Even then there remained the problem of how Lewis could avoid the "scandal" of taking into his house a woman to whom he had not been united by the Christian sacrament of marriage, albeit one who was sadly dying of cancer. After talking the matter over with the Bishop of Oxford, Lewis turned to an old friend, Father Peter Bide, of the Diocese of London. Father Bide had, he told Walter Hooper, healed several people by the laying on of hands. On March 21, 1957, he came down to Oxford to lay his hands on Joy Davidman: afterwards—because it seemed the right thing to do—he married Lewis and Joy in the Wingfield-Morris hospital. But all this is explained so much better and

Lewis at The Kilns, 1958

A drawing Juliet Pannett made of Lewis in Magdalene
College, Cambridge, on February 7, 1963, first published in
The Illustrated London News of July 27, 1963

tenderly, in a letter Lewis wrote to Dorothy L. Sayers on June 25, 1957:

"I ought to tell you my own news. On examination it turned out that Joy's previous marriage, made in her pre-Christian days, was no marriage: the man had a wife still living. The Bishop of Oxford said it was not the present policy to approve re-marriage in such cases ... Then dear Father Bide (do you know him?) who had come to lay his hands on Joy—for he has on his record what looks v. like one miracle —without being asked and merely on being told the situation at once

The driveway leading to The Kilns

said he wd. marry us. So we had a bedside marriage with a nuptial Mass. When I last wrote to you I could not even have wished this: you will gather (and may say 'guessed as much') that my feelings had changed. They say a rival often turns a friend into a lover. Thanatos, certainly (they say) approaching but at an uncertain speed, is a most efficient rival for this purpose. We soon learn to love what we know we must love. I hope you give us your blessing: I know you'll give us your prayers. She is home now, not because she is better (tho' in fact she *seems* amazingly better) but because they can do no more for her at the

Wingfield; totally bed-ridden but—you'd be surprised—we have much gaiety and even some happiness. Indeed, the situation is not easy to describe. My heart is breaking and I was never so happy before; at any rate there is more in life than I knew about. My own personal pains lately (which were among the severest I've known) had an odd element of relief in them."[8]

The pains Lewis suffered were caused by osteoporosis, which in his case resulted from a loss of calcium in the bones. At the same time his pains began to increase, the doctors found the cancer disappearing

The building which served as the Lewis garage, but which dates back to the 1880s when it was used by those making bricks on this site. August 1963

On the left a nineteenth-century shed for brick-making; *right,*
the greenhouse of The Kilns. August 1963

from Joy's body. Indeed, it was the doctors who, on the evidence of X-rays, pronounced her recovery to be a "miracle." At the time, the regular staff of The Kilns consisted of Fred Paxford, the gardener who had been with Lewis since 1930, Mrs. Molly Miller, the housekeeper since 1952, and a housemaid. When Joy originally came to live at The Kilns there had been three full-time nurses to look after her, but by the autumn of 1957 they were no longer needed. Indeed, such was her recovery that by the summer of 1958 Lewis and Joy were able to dine with Nevill Coghill in Merton College. Recalling the event, Professor Coghill wrote: "Shortly after Lewis's marriage, when he brought his wife to lunch with me, he said to me, looking at her across the grassy quadrangle, 'I never expected to have, in my sixties, the happiness that passed me by in my twenties.' It was then that he told me of having been allowed to accept her pain.

" 'You mean' (I said) 'that the pain left her, and that you felt it for her in your body?'

" 'Yes,' he said, 'in my legs. It was crippling. But it relieved hers.' "[9]

As Lewis could not neglect his duties at Cambridge, he gave a number of dinner parties at both Oxford and Cambridge so that his friends and colleagues could meet Joy and (hopefully) provide her with company when he was away. Joy was to make a number of friends, particularly Warnie, who liked her very much and upon whom she exercised a totally good influence: his drinking was curtailed for a while and he took more interest in his books about the reign of Louis XIV possibly because of Joy's enthusiasm for this period in French history. Still, most of those who met her acted with less than enthusiasm, finding her too "brassy" for their taste. If she was aware of this, it seems not to have spoiled her and Lewis's happiness, which was hard won and which had grown from adversity.

Lewis at The Kilns with the author

In July 1958 they flew (Lewis's first experience of an airplane) to Ireland for a fortnight's travelling holiday with Arthur Greeves. When Lewis was at Cambridge Joy found extraordinary happiness in such ordinary things as decorating The Kilns (which had become somewhat squalid since Mrs. Moore's death) and proof-reading, amongst other books, Lewis's *Till We Have Faces* (1956) and *Reflections on the Psalms* (1958). Then the Damocles sword which had long hung over them made itself known. It had been Joy's life-long ambition to visit Greece, and it was while this was under discussion that some X-rays made in October 1959 revealed a new outbreak of cancer in several parts of her body. "This last check," Lewis wrote to Roger Lancelyn Green in November, "is the only one we approached without dread—her health seemed so complete. It is like being recaptured by the Giant when you have passed

Maureen, Lady Dunbar of Hempriggs, in the "Morning Room" of her castle in Scotland, August 1965

Paxford and the cat "Tom" in the kitchen. The Kilns, August 1963

every gate and are almost out of sight of his castle. Whether a second miracle will be vouchsafed us, or, if not, when the sentence will be inflicted, remains uncertain. It is quite possible she may be able to do the Greek trip next spring. Pray for us."[10]

Lewis took little interest in foreign travel, but for Joy's sake—because she desired it so fervently—it was decided they would tour Greece with their friends Roger and June Lancelyn Green. He was, nevertheless, very apprehensive when the taxi arrived to take them to the airport. Recalling those anxious moments a few years later, he told Walter Hooper with some mirth of Paxford's parting words: meant so kindly but which sounded so full of doom at the time. Paxford was very fond of listening to the wire-less (radio). Leaning through the window of the taxi, he said "Well, Mr. Jack, there was this bloke just going on

Mrs. Molly Miller, housekeeper at The Kilns, August 1963

over the wire-less. Says an airplane just went down. Everybody killed —burnt beyond recognition. Did you hear what I said, Mr. Jack? *Burnt beyond recognition!*"

The trip through the isles of Greece with the Lancelyn Greens between April 3 and 14, 1960, problematic though it seemed before they set out, was for all of them happy almost beyond the bearing of it. This memorable experience was recorded in Roger's diary and can be found in full in *C. S. Lewis: A Biography* (1974) by Roger Lancelyn Green and Walter Hooper.

They returned in such a happy frame of mind that Joy's slow and peaceful decline was almost without anguish. Early on the morning of July 13, 1960, Warnie, whose room was over Joy's, was wakened by her screaming. Lewis was able to secure a private room for her in the Radcliffe Infirmary. Except for the minutes during which the Hospital Chaplain heard her confession and granted absolution, he remained with her for the rest of the day. "I am at peace with God" were her last words before she died that evening about 10 o'clock.

As so often, pen and ink proved a means of consolation for Lewis. During the months following Joy's death he poured his feelings into a partly autobiographical work published under the pseudonym N. W. Clerk as *A Grief Observed* (1961). It has proved to be of immense consolation to those who, in losing husband, wife, or friend, have felt spiritually bankrupt, yet found their faith strengthened in the end. But it does not duplicate exactly Lewis's own highly unusual marriage. It was not meant to. For religious as well as physical reasons Lewis's marriage was not consummated. Lewis's grief and, in the end, resolution, are of course there. Even so, the book was intended for "Everyman," and in order to achieve this Lewis felt he had to add certain "paddings" if the book was to be of help to the average man and woman.

Lewis had neglected his own health during Joy's last years; now these old neglects were beginning to take their revenge. When Arthur visited him in June 1961 he was distressed to find him looking so ill. Following the visit Lewis went to the doctors, who discovered a distended prostate gland. An operation was scheduled but it had to be postponed, as Lewis was having trouble with his kidneys as well and an operation would have been too dangerous to his heart. In the end, he was fitted with a catheter, put on a low-protein diet, and for the remainder of his life required occasional blood transfusions. "I'd write more," he said to the poet Kathleen Raine on October 25, 1961, "but I've just had a blood transfusion and am feeling drowsy. Dracula must have led a horrid life!"[11]

Having not an iota of the hypochondriac in him, Lewis tended to be rather bored with the state of his health. He regretted being unable to take the long walks he was so fond of; and though the low-protein diet was a nuisance, he never grumbled. "We Lewises burn out quickly," he once remarked to Professor Basil Willey.[12] When he returned to Cambridge he was anxious not to be a burden to the college servants, telling them that at High Table he would eat whatever was allowable. But they liked him too well for this and the college chef insisted on preparing dishes specially for him.

In spite of his illness he carried on with his lecturing and writing. It was during 1960–62 that he collected some of his miscellaneous

Mrs. Miller, her sister, the housemaid, and Douglas Gresham
in the kitchen of The Kilns, August 1963

essays into *They Asked for a Paper* (1962), turned his Prolegomena
lectures into what would be *The Discarded Image,* and resumed work
on a book abandoned in 1953—*Letters to Malcolm: Chiefly on Prayer*
(1964). His relish for pastime with good company was unimpaired and
the Monday Inklings were continued, albeit in the "Lamb and Flag"
pub as the old Bird and Baby had been "modernised."

It was in the spring of 1963 that he was to make a new friend whom
he was to speak of as "the son I should have had."[13] This was the North
Carolinian, Walter Hooper, then lecturing on English literature at the
University of Kentucky. After several years of corresponding, Lewis
invited him over for a visit. Hooper's arrival at The Kilns coincided

with one of Warnie's longest holidays in Ireland. Hooper recalls that after ringing the doorbell on his first visit to meet the man he had so long idolised he was overtaken by such terror that he could see his heart thumping beneath his coat. Should he stay or run? *Could* he run? Footsteps within signaled that it was too late. Inside, however, Lewis quickly put him at his ease. After two hours' talk, Lewis took him off for a drink at his favourite local, "The Ampleforth Arms." Hooper assumed that this was to be his only visit and when he began thanking him for his hospitality Lewis said, "But won't I see you again? You're not getting away! Meet me at the Lamb and Flag on Monday as I want to talk with you some more."

Warnie Lewis taking tea with the author at 19 Beaumont Street

After this they settled into a regular routine of thrice-weekly meet-ings: Mondays at the Lamb and Flag, Thursdays at The Kilns, and on Sundays they attended early Mass together at Lewis's parish church. As in all friendships, the reasons why two people find so much pleasure in one another's company must always remain something of a mystery. No one is the worse for that. For whatever reasons, the older and the younger man simply liked one another. The jokes which emerged from their different nationalities may have contributed to this. "It took some time for an American," wrote Hooper, "to adapt to English 'conve-niences.' I see . . . from my diary . . . that during a longish visit with Lewis we drank what seemed gallons of tea. After a while I asked to be shown the 'bathroom,' forgetting that in most homes the bathroom and the toilet are separate rooms. With a kind of mock formality, Lewis showed me to the bathroom, pointed to the tub, flung down a pile of towels, and closed the door behind me. I returned to his sitting-room to say that it was not a *bath* I wanted but . . . 'Well, sir, "choose you this day," ' said Lewis, bursting with laughter as he quoted the prophet Joshua, '*that* will break you of those silly American euphemisms. And now, *where* is it you wanted to go?' "[14]

For some time Lewis had been planning a short holiday in Ireland with his step-son, Douglas, and Arthur Greeves. However, when Hooper arrived to take him to Mass on July 14 Lewis was too ill to leave the house. Recognising his need for help, and in particular someone to assist him with his vast correspondence, it was then that he urged Hooper to become his companion-secretary and move into The Kilns. The next day Lewis went for a routine examination at the Acland Nurs-ing Home, and, much to everyone's surprise, he sank into a coma lasting about twenty-four hours. The doctors did not believe he would recover, and a priest was called in to administer Extreme Unction. Remarkably, he did recover and it was during his stay in the nursing home that he asked Walter Hooper to move into The Kilns and spend the days with him talking and taking dictation.

Walter Hooper remembers this stay in the nursing home as being a time when Lewis was full of jollity and high spirits. But there were a few days when, because of his illness, Lewis's mind was disordered. It was on one of these days that he was unable to recognise any of those who dropped in to see him—not even Professor Tolkien. Hooper watched despairingly until one visitor arrived whose effect on Lewis was very like stepping into the world of Narnia. "The last visitor of the day," Hooper recalls, "was his foster-sister, Maureen Moore Blake, who a few months previously, and by a very unexpected turn of events, had become Lady Dunbar of Hempriggs, with a castle and a vast estate in Scotland. She was the first woman in three centuries to succeed to a baronetcy. They had not met since this happened and, hoping to spare her any disappointment, I told her that he had not been able to recognise any of his old friends. He opened his eyes when she took his hand. 'Jack,' she whispered, 'it is Maureen.' 'No,' replied Lewis smiling, 'it is Lady Dunbar of Hempriggs.' 'Oh, Jack, how could you remember that?' she asked. 'On the contrary,' he said. 'How could *I* forget a fairy tale?' "

When he was allowed home on August 6 he seemed fit. Even so, he felt it only fair to his colleagues at Cambridge that he resign his chair. Sometime later he wrote to the Master of Magdalene College, Sir Henry Willink, saying, "The ghosts of the wicked old women in Pope 'haunt the places where their honour died.' I am more fortunate, for I shall haunt the place whence the most valued of my honours came. I am constantly with you in imagination. If in some twilit hour anyone sees

Lewis never spared the time to sit for an oil portrait. As a result, this bronze bust, sculpted in 1980 by Faith Tolkien (daughter-in-law of J. R.R. Tolkien) was commissioned by Walter Hooper and donated to Magdalen College to serve as an Oxford memorial to one loved by so many.

Lewis in the "common room" of The Kilns shortly before his
retirement, August 1963

a bald and bulky spectre in the Combination Room or the garden, don't
get Simon [Barrington-Ward—the Chaplain] to exorcise it, for it is a
harmless wraith, and means nothing but good."[15]

During that summer he seemed to his secretary remarkably unlike
a wraith. After his totally unexpected recovery in the Acland the doctors were cautious with their diagnosis. They said that while there was
a strong possibility that he might live for years, he could die at any
moment. "I see myself," he told Hooper, "as a sentinel on duty. I'm
willing to stay until I'm called—but, mind, I would sooner be called."
And to Sister Penelope he was to write: "I was unexpectedly revived
from a long coma—and perhaps the almost continuous prayers of my

friends did it—but it would have been a luxuriously easy passage and one almost . . . regrets having the door shut in one's face. Ought we to honour Lazarus rather than Stephen as the protomartyr? To be brought back and have all one's dying to do *again* was rather hard. When you die, and if 'prison visiting' is allowed, come down and look me up in Purgatory. It *is* all rather fun—solemn fun—isn't it?"[16]

Meanwhile, as it appeared that Jack Lewis would live for several more years, he and Walter got on with their work, the Monday morning Inklings meetings, the pints of beer, the steady conversations over cups of tea, visits from friends, and all the rest. They were happy times indeed, with Paxford the gardener and Mrs. Miller, and most of all, Jack with his irrepressible fun.

Lewis at his desk in the "common room" of The Kilns, August 1963

He always sent Mrs. Miller home after dinner, and it never occurred to Hooper who might be washing the dishes till, one evening, he followed Lewis into the kitchen and found him in the scullery up to his arms in soap-suds. Then, sensing that Hooper was astounded to discover that the author of *The Screwtape Letters* also washed dishes, he said, laughing, "If ever you tell others what it is like in this house, you must say that not only are the servants soft underfoot but *invisible* as well!"

Hooper recalls that moving into The Kilns deprived him of saying "As C. S. Lewis has said," something which Hooper enjoyed immensely. Occasionally, though, he forgot himself and said it to Lewis directly.

> "As C. S. Lewis has said—oh, I'm sorry, you *are* C. S. Lewis aren't you?"
> "Yes I am."

Then Lewis saw that two could play that game. "As C. S. Lewis has said," *he* would say, "we ought to have some tea. As C. S. Lewis has said, '*You* make it.' As C. S. Lewis has said, '*I* will drink it.' "

Then in September Hooper had to go back to the United States to sort out his affairs before returning after Christmas to resume his duties as Lewis's secretary. Little did he know that he had already enjoyed (except for the full-grown pleasure of remembering) the most glorious months of his life.

Lewis's anxiety for his loved brother, Warnie, was set to rest when, in October, Warnie returned from Ireland to look after him. As in the old days at Little Lea when elder brother looked after younger brother, so Warnie was to do again with great tenderness. Of the last few weeks in The Kilns together Warnie was to write:

Once again—as in the earliest days—we could turn for comfort only to each other. The Wheel had come full circle: once again we were together in the little end room at home, shutting out from our talk the ever-present knowledge that the holidays were ending, that a new term fraught with unknown possibilities awaited us both.

Jack faced the prospect bravely and calmly. "I have done all I wanted to do, and I'm ready to go," he said to me one evening. Only once did he show any regret or reluctance: this was when I told him that the morning's mail included an invitation to deliver the Romanes lecture. An expression of sadness passed over his face, and there was a moment's silence: then, "Send them a very polite refusal."

Our talk tended to be cheerfully reminiscent during these last days: long-forgotten incidents in our shared past would be remembered, and the old Jack would return for a moment, whimsical and witty. We were recapturing the old schoolboy technique of extracting the last drop of juice from our holidays.

Friday, the 22nd of November 1963, began much as other days: there was breakfast, then letters and the crossword puzzle. After lunch he fell asleep in his chair: I suggested that he would be more comfortable in bed, and he went there. At four I took in his tea and found him drowsy but comfortable. Our few words then were the last: at five-thirty I heard a crash and ran in, to find him lying unconscious at the foot of his bed. He ceased to breathe some three or four minutes later. The following Friday would have been his sixty-fifth birthday.[17]

Lewis's gravestone in the churchyard of Holy Trinity Church, Headington Quarry

Three days later his body was taken to his parish church in Headington Quarry where it lay overnight. The next morning, November 26, a Requiem Mass was said by his priest. The funeral followed shortly afterwards and was attended by most of the Inklings and other of his friends. "There was one candle on the coffin," recalls Peter Bayley, "as it was carried out into the churchyard. It seemed not only appropriate but almost a symbol of the man and his integrity and his absoluteness and his faith that the flame burned so steadily, even in the open air, and seemed so bright, even in the bright sun." "Certainly we have lost a friend," Commander Dundas-Grant whispered to Dr. Havard. To which the latter replied, "Only for a time."[18]

"Then Aslan turned to them and said: '. . . you are—as you used to call it in the Shadowlands—dead. The term is over: the holidays have begun. The dream is ended: this is the morning . . .'

"And for us this is the end of all the stories, and we can most truly say that they all lived happily ever after. But for them it was only the beginning of the real story. All their life in this world and all their adventures in Narnia had only been the cover and the title page: now at last they were beginning Chapter One of the Great Story which no one on earth has read: which goes on forever: in which every chapter is better than the one before."

NOTES

PART I

1. *Surprised by Joy: The Shape of My Early Life* (London, 1955; New York, 1956), ch. X, p. 148.
2. *Ibid.*, ch. I, p. 11.
3. *Lewis Papers*, vol. II, p. 248 (original of *Papers* in Wheaton College, Illinois; copy in Bodleian Library).
4. *Ibid.*, vol. I, p. 5.
5. *Surprised by Joy*, ch. I, p. 17.
6. *Ibid.*, pp. 21–22.
7. *The Locked Door.*
8. *The Sailor.*
9. Unpublished "Biography of C. S. Lewis" by W. H. Lewis.
10. *Surprised by Joy*, ch. I, pp. 21–23.
11. *Ibid.*, p. 25.
12. *Ibid.*, p. 27.
13. *Ibid.*, pp. 38–39.
14. *Lewis Papers*, vol. III, p. 194.
15. *Surprised by Joy*, ch. VIII, pp. 117–119.
16. *Ibid.*, ch. III, p. 55.
17. *They Stand Together: the Letters of C. S. Lewis to Arthur Greeves (1914–1963)*, ed. Walter Hooper (London; New York, 1979), p. 10.
18. *Surprised by Joy*, ch. V, pp. 74–75.
19. *Ibid.*, ch. I, pp. 23–24.
20. *Ibid.*, ch. XI, p. 161.
21. Charles Wrong, "A Chance Meeting," *C. S. Lewis at the Breakfast Table and Other Reminiscences*, ed. James T. Como (New York; London, 1979), pp. 112–113.
22. *Surprised by Joy*, ch. VIII, p. 125.
23. *Ibid.*, pp. 125–126.
24. *They Stand Together*, p. 25.
25. *Surprised by Joy*, ch. IX, pp. 130–131.
26. *Letters of C. S. Lewis*, ed. with a Memoir by W. H. Lewis (London; New York, 1966), pp. 5–6.

PART II

1. *They Stand Together*, letter of April 28, 1917, p. 179.
2. *Ibid.*, pp. 179–180.
3. *Ibid.*, letter of July 8, 1917, pp. 194–195.
4. *Lewis Papers*, vol. V, pp. 241–242.
5. *Surprised by Joy*, ch. XII, pp. 184–185.
6. Leo Baker, "Near the Beginning," *C. S. Lewis at the Breakfast Table and Other Reminiscences*, p. 5.
7. Letter of Lord Byron to his mother from Harrow, May 1–10, 1804.
8. *They Stand Together*, p. 135.
9. *Lewis Papers*, vol. VI, p. 123.
10. *Ibid.*, p. 145.
11. *Letters of C. S. Lewis*, p. 13.
12. Hester Lynch Thrale Piozzi, *Anecdotes of the Late Samuel Johnson* (1786), p. 298.
13. *Letters of C. S. Lewis*, letter of March 31, 1928, p. 125.
14. *Ibid.*, p. 48.

15. Bodleian Library, MS. Top. Oxon. d. 95/1, fol. 72.
16. *Ibid.*, fol. 109.
17. MS. Top. Oxon. d. 95/2, fol. 44.
18. *Letters of C. S. Lewis*, p. 90.
19. *Lewis Papers*, vol. VIII, p. 299.
20. Letter to Publisher on the original dust jacket of the American edition of *Perelandra* (New York, 1944).
21. *They Stand Together*, p. 305.
22. *Ibid.*, p. 306.
23. *Ibid.*
24. *Letters of C. S. Lewis*, p. 21.
25. *They Stand Together*, pp. 472–474.
26. Letter of Lord Byron to Thomas Moore from Venice, March 31, 1817.
27. *Surprised by Joy*, ch. XIV, p. 211.
28. Undated letter to Owen Barfield (c. 1929), copies of which are in the Bodleian Library and Wheaton College, Illinois.
29. *Surprised by Joy*, ch. XIV, p. 215.
30. *They Stand Together*, p. 427.
31. *Surprised by Joy*, ch. XV, pp. 223–224.

PART III

1. *The Times Literary Supplement* (June 6, 1936), p. 475.
2. *Letters of C. S. Lewis*, pp. 170–171 (the entire text of which letter can be found in the Bodleian Library and in Wheaton College, Illinois).
3. *Ibid.*, p. 177.
4. *Ibid.*, 178.
5. *Mere Christianity* (London; New York, 1952), Bk. II, ch. 3, p. 42.
6. For a full account of Lewis's part in the Socratic Club see Walter Hooper's "Oxford's Bonny Fighter" in *C. S. Lewis at the Breakfast Table and Other Reminiscences*.
7. In C. S. Lewis's *Transposition and Other Addresses* (London, 1949), pp. 52–53. The same book published as *The Weight of Glory and Other Addresses* (New York, 1949), pp. 14–15.
8. *Letters of C. S. Lewis*, p. 188.
9. *The Screwtape Letters* (London, 1942; New York, 1943), Letter 12.
10. Preface to *The Screwtape Letters and Screwtape Proposes a Toast* (London, 1961; New York, 1962), p. 12.
11. "Mr. Lewis's Devil," *New Statesman and Nation*, vol. XXIII (May 16, 1942), p. 324.

PART IV

1. *They Stand Together*, p. 519.
2. Letter from Basil Willey to Walter Hooper of September 20, 1970. Bodleian Library.
3. Bodleian Library with copy in Wheaton College.
4. Richard W. Ladborough, "In Cambridge," *C. S. Lewis at the Breakfast Table and Other Reminiscences*, pp. 99–103.
5. *They Stand Together*, p. 534.
6. *Ibid.*, p. 543.
7. Copy in the Bodleian Library.
8. Copy in the Bodleian Library.
9. Nevill Coghill, "The Approach to English," *Light on C. S. Lewis*, ed. Jocelyn Gibb (London, 1965; New York, 1966), p. 63.
10. Roger Lancelyn Green and Walter Hooper, *C. S. Lewis: A Biography* (1974), p. 270.
11. Bodleian Library with copy at Wheaton College.
12. Letter from Basil Willey to Walter Hooper of September 20, 1970. Bodleian Library.
13. *C. S. Lewis: A Biography*, Ch. XII, p. 303.

14. C. S. Lewis, *The Weight of Glory and Other Addresses*, Revised and Expanded Edition, edited with an Introduction by Walter Hooper (New York, 1980), pp. x–xi.
15. *Letters of C. S. Lewis*, p. 308.
16. *Ibid.*, p. 307.
17. *Letters of C. S. Lewis*, "Memoir" by W. H. Lewis, pp. 24–25.
18. Peter Bayley, "From Master to Colleague," and James Dundas-Grant, "From An 'Outsider,' " in *C. S. Lewis at the Breakfast Table*, p. 86, p. 233.

The Books of C. S. Lewis

This bibliography is confined to titles, publishers, and dates of publication. Some of the books are collections of essays, poems, and letters published prior to their appearance in book form. Those interested in a more detailed list of Lewis's published writings are advised to see my "Bibliography of the Writings of C. S. Lewis" in *C. S. Lewis at the Breakfast Table and Other Reminiscences*, ed. James T. Como (New York, 1979; London, 1980). American editions are in brackets except where there is no English edition. Place of publication is London or New York respectively if no place is given. —W.H.

Spirits in Bondage: A Cycle of Lyrics. London: William Heinemann, 1919 (under the pseudonym of Clive Hamilton).

Dymer. London: J. M. Dent, 1926 (under the pseudonym of Clive Hamilton); reprinted with a new Preface, as by C. S. Lewis, by J. M. Dent for Dent *and* Macmillan of New York, 1950 [E. P. Dutton, 1926].

The Pilgrim's Regress: An Allegorical Apology for Christianity, Reason and Romanticism. London: J. M. Dent, 1933; Sheed and Ward, 1935; Geoffrey Bles, 1943, with the author's new Preface on Romanticism, footnotes, and running headlines [Sheed and Ward, 1944; Grand Rapids: Eerdmans, 1958].

The Allegory of Love: A Study in Medieval Tradition. Oxford: Clarendon Press, 1936; reprinted with corrections, London: Oxford University Press, 1938 [Oxford University Press, 1958].

Out of the Silent Planet. London: John Lane the Bodley Head, 1938 [Macmillan, 1943].

Rehabilitations and Other Essays. London: Oxford University Press, 1939.

(With E. M. W. Tillyard) *The Personal Heresy: A Controversy*. London: Oxford University Press, 1939.

The Problem of Pain. London: The Centenary Press, 1940 [Macmillan, 1943].

The Screwtape Letters. London: Geoffrey Bles, 1942 [Macmillan, 1943]; reprinted with a new Screwtape letter as *The Screwtape Letters and Screwtape Proposes a Toast*, with a new and additional Preface, London: Geoffrey Bles, 1961 [Macmillan, 1962].

A Preface to "Paradise Lost": Being the Ballard Matthews Lectures Delivered at University College, North Wales, 1941, Revised and Enlarged. London: Oxford University Press, 1942.

Broadcast Talks: Reprinted with some alterations from two series of Broadcast Talks ("Right and Wrong: A Clue to the Meaning of the Universe" and "What Christians Believe") given in 1941 and 1942. London: Geoffrey Bles: The Centenary Press, 1942 [As *The Case for Christianity*, Macmillan, 1943].

Christian Behaviour: A further series of Broadcast Talks. London: Geoffrey Bles: The Centenary Press, 1943 [Macmillan, 1943].

Perelandra. London: John Lane the Bodley Head, 1943 [Macmillan, 1944].

The Abolition of Man: or Reflections on Education with Special Reference to the Teaching of English in the Upper Forms of Schools. London: Oxford University Press, 1943; with some alterations, London: Geoffrey Bles: The Centenary Press, 1946 [Macmillan, 1947].

Beyond Personality: The Christian Idea of God. London: Geoffrey Bles: The Centenary Press, 1944 [Macmillan, 1945].

That Hideous Strength: A Modern Fairy-tale for Grown-ups. London: John Lane the Bodley Head, 1945 [Macmillan, 1946].

The Great Divorce: A Dream. London: Geoffrey Bles: The Centenary Press, 1945 [Macmillan, 1946].

Miracles: A Preliminary Study. London: Geoffrey Bles: The Centenary Press, 1947 [Macmillan, 1947]. With revision of Chapter III, London: Collins, 1960 [Macmillan, 1978].

Arthurian Torso: Containing the Posthumous Fragment of "The Figure of Arthur" by Charles Williams and A Commentary on the Arthurian Poems of Charles Williams by C. S. Lewis. London: Oxford University Press, 1948 [Contained in *Taliessin Through Logres, The Region of the Summer Stars by Charles Williams and Arthurian Torso by Charles Williams and C. S. Lewis.* Grand Rapids: Eerdmans, 1974].

Transposition and Other Addresses. London: Geoffrey Bles, 1949 [As *The Weight of Glory and Other Addresses,* Macmillan, 1949; Revised and Expanded Edition, ed. Walter Hooper, Macmillan, 1980].

The Lion, the Witch and the Wardrobe: A Story for Children. Illustrations by Pauline Baynes. London: Geoffrey Bles, 1950 [Macmillan, 1950].

Prince Caspian: The Return to Narnia. Illustrations by Pauline Baynes. London: Geoffrey Bles, 1951 [Macmillan, 1951].

Mere Christianity: A revised and amplified edition, with a new introduction, of the three books "Broadcast Talks," "Christian Behaviour," and "Beyond Personality." London: Geoffrey Bles, 1952 [As *Mere Christianity: A revised and enlarged edition, with a new introduction, of the three books "The Case for Christianity," "Christian Behaviour," and "Beyond Personality,"* Macmillan, 1952; *Mere Christianity: An Anniversary Edition,* with additional broadcasts by C. S. Lewis, ed. Walter Hooper, Macmillan, 1981].

The Voyage of the "Dawn Treader." Illustrations by Pauline Baynes. London: Geoffrey Bles, 1952 [Macmillan, 1952].

The Silver Chair. Illustrations by Pauline Baynes. London: Geoffrey Bles, 1953 [Macmillan, 1953].

The Horse and His Boy. Illustrations by Pauline Baynes. London: Geoffrey Bles, 1954 [Macmillan, 1954].

English Literature in the Sixteenth Century, excluding Drama. Oxford: Clarendon Press, 1954.

The Magician's Nephew. Illustrations by Pauline Baynes. London: The Bodley Head, 1955 [Macmillan, 1955].

Surprised by Joy: The Shape of My Early Life. London: Geoffrey Bles, 1955 [Harcourt, Brace & World, 1956].

The Last Battle: A Story for Children. Illustrations by Pauline Baynes. London: The Bodley Head, 1956 [Macmillan, 1956].

Till We Have Faces: A Myth Retold. London: Geoffrey Bles, 1956 [Harcourt, Brace & World, 1957].

Reflections on the Psalms. London: Geoffrey Bles, 1958 [Harcourt, Brace & World, 1958].

The Four Loves. London: Geoffrey Bles, 1960 [Harcourt, Brace & World, 1960].

Studies in Words. Cambridge: Cambridge University Press, 1960; the Second Edition includes three new chapters, 1967.

The World's Last Night and Other Essays. New York: Harcourt, Brace & World, 1960.

A Grief Observed. London: Faber and Faber, 1961 (under the pseudonym of N. W. Clerk); reprinted, as by C. S. Lewis, 1964 [Greenwich, Connecticut: Seabury Press, 1963 (under the pseudonym of N. W. Clerk)].

An Experiment in Criticism. Cambridge: Cambridge University Press, 1961.

They Asked for a Paper: Papers and Addresses. London: Geoffrey Bles, 1962.

Letters to Malcolm: Chiefly on Prayer. London: Geoffrey Bles, 1964 [Harcourt, Brace & World, 1964].

The Discarded Image: An Introduction to Medieval and Renaissance Literature. Cambridge: Cambridge University Press, 1964.

Poems. ed. Walter Hooper. London: Geoffrey Bles, 1964 [Harcourt, Brace & World, 1965].

Screwtape Proposes a Toast and Other Pieces. London: Collins, 1965.

Studies in Medieval and Renaissance Literature. ed. Walter Hooper. Cambridge: Cambridge University Press, 1966.

Letters of C. S. Lewis. ed. with a Memoir by W. H. Lewis. London: Geoffrey Bles, 1966 [Harcourt, Brace & World, 1966].

Of Other Worlds: Essays and Stories. ed. Walter Hooper. London: Geoffrey Bles, 1966 [Harcourt, Brace & World, 1967].

Christian Reflections. ed. Walter Hooper. London: Geoffrey Bles, 1967 [Grand Rapids: Eerdmans, 1967].

Spenser's Images of Life. ed. Alastair Fowler. Cambridge: Cambridge University Press, 1967.

A Mind Awake: An Anthology of C. S. Lewis. ed. Clyde S. Kilby. London: Geoffrey Bles, 1968 [Harcourt, Brace & World, 1969].

Narrative Poems. ed. Walter Hooper. London: Geoffrey Bles, 1969 [Harcourt Brace Jovanovich, 1972].

Selected Literary Essays. ed. Walter Hooper. Cambridge: Cambridge University Press, 1969.

God in the Dock: Essays on Theology and Ethics. ed. Walter Hooper. Grand Rapids: Eerdmans, 1970 (As *Undeceptions: Essays on Theology and Ethics*, London: Geoffrey Bles, 1971).

Fern-Seed and Elephants and Other Essays on Christianity. ed. Walter Hooper. London: Collins, 1975.

The Dark Tower and Other Stories. ed. Walter Hooper. London: Collins, 1977 [Harcourt Brace Jovanovich, 1977].

The Joyful Christian: 127 Readings from C. S. Lewis. ed. Henry William Griffin. New York: Macmillan, 1977.

God in the Dock: Essays on Theology. ed. Walter Hooper. London: Collins, 1979.

They Stand Together: The Letters of C. S. Lewis to Arthur Greeves (1914–1963). ed. Walter Hooper. London: Collins, 1979 [Macmillan, 1979].

The Visionary Christian: 131 Readings from C. S. Lewis. ed. Chad Walsh. New York: Macmillan, 1981.

On Stories and Other Essays on Literature. ed. Walter Hooper. New York: Harcourt Brace Jovanovich, 1982 (As *Of This and Other Worlds*, London: Collins, 1982).

Sources of Illustrations

I am grateful to all who have allowed me to reproduce the illustrations contained in this book. In order to make this information clear, each acknowledgment is divided into three (or in some instances, two) sections, separated by a colon. The information is given in the following order: (1) a brief description of the photograph or artistic work; (2) the name, if known, of the photographer or artist who made the work; and (3) the person or institution who owns or commissioned it. The photograph on page 2 can be taken as an example:

p. 2   The Mountains of Mourne: Bob O'Donnell: Lord and King Associates

When, however, the photographer and the owner of the copyright are the same it has not been thought necessary to duplicate this information. An example of this is as follows:

p. ii   CSL in Magdalen College: A. P. Strong

All photographs made by Bob O'Donnell and Billett Potter copyright MCMLXXIX by Lord and King Associates, Inc.

p. 18   Flora with children: unknown: Estate of W. H. Lewis

p. 20   Little Lea: unknown: Bodleian Library

p. 21   Entrance hall of Little Lea: Bob O'Donnell: Lord and King
        Walter Hooper in Little Lea: Bob O'Donnell: Lord and King

p. 22   Walter Hooper in "little end room": Bob O'Donnell: Lord and King

p. 23   "Lord Big": C. S. Lewis: Estate of C. S. Lewis

p. 24   Wynyard School: Jeffrey Whitelaw

p. 25   Schoolroom of Wynyard School: unknown: Walter Hooper

p. 26   Christmas party at Little Lea: Augustus Hamilton: Bodleian Library
        Albert Lewis and his sons: unknown: Estate of W. H. Lewis

p. 27   Tennis party at Glenmachan: Gundreda Ewart: Bodleian Library

p. 28   Jack, Warren, and Albert Lewis with W. H. Patterson: unknown: Bodleian Library

p. 29   Jack, Albert, and Warren: unknown: Estate of W. H. Lewis
        Campbell College: Bob O'Donnell: Lord and King
        Cherbourg School: Bob O'Donnell: Lord and King

p. 30   Boys of Cherbourg School: Norman May of Malvern: Walter Hooper

p. 31   Cherbourg School theatrical: unknown: Bodleian Library

p. 32   Gundreda Ewart: unknown: Mrs. Primrose Henderson
        Glenmachan House: Bob O'Donnell: Lord and King
        Malvern College: Bob O'Donnell: Lord and King

p. 33   Malvern College dormitory: Bob O'Donnell: Lord and King
        "Bernagh": Bob O'Donnell: Lord and King

p. 34   Arthur Greeves: unknown: Mrs. Lisbeth Greeves
        Painting by Arthur Greeves: Anderson-McMeekin of Belfast: Mrs. Lisbeth Greeves

p. 35   Mr. and Mrs. W. T. Kirkpatrick: W. H. Lewis: Bodleian Library
        Barn at "Gastons": Billett Potter: Lord and King

p. 36   Afternoon tea at "Bernagh": unknown: Bodleian Library

p. 40   Spires of Oxford: Bob O'Donnell: Lord and King

p. 42   University College: A. F. Kersting: Christopher Hobhouse, *Oxford* (1939)

p. 43   Front quad of University College: Billett Potter: Lord and King
        University College members of 1917: unknown: University College

p. 44   "Parson's Pleasure": Lancelot Speed: *Aspects of Modern Oxford by a Mere Don* (1894)

p. 45   University College used as a hospital: unknown: Bodleian Library

p. 46   Smoking room of Oxford Union: T. H. Crawford: *Aspects of Modern Oxford*
        Examination Schools as hospital: unknown: Bodleian Library

p. 47   Mrs. Moore's home in Bristol: Billett Potter: Lord and King
        Hillsboro House: Billett Potter: Lord and King

p. 48   Oxford O.T.C. cadets: unknown: Bodleian Library

p. 49   CSL and "Paddy" Moore: unknown: Bodleian Library

p. 50   CSL with father: Abernethy of Belfast: Walter Hooper

p. 51   Jack and Albert Lewis: W. H. Lewis: Bodleian Library
        CSL after return from war: unknown: Walter Hooper

p. 52   University College members of 1919: unknown: University College

p. 53   CSL in "little end room": W. H. Lewis: Bodleian Library
        Albert Lewis in study: W. H. Lewis: Bodleian Library

p. 54   The Kilns in 1930: W. H. Lewis: Bodleian Library
        Wardrobe carved by R. Lewis: Bob O'Donnell: Lord and King

Index

Rather than provide a separate list of the many photographs in this book, all photographs are indicated by numbers printed in bold figures.